IRON HORSE PRIZE

KATIE CORTESE, SERIES EDITOR

Also in the series:
The Birthright of Sons: Stories
by Jefferey Spivey

Sing with Me at the Edge of Paradise: Stories
by Joe Baumann

LUCKY BODIES

ESSAYS

MARIANNE
JAY ERHARDT

TEXAS TECH UNIVERSITY PRESS

This book is typeset in Adobe Caslon Pro. The paper used in this book meets the minimum requirements of ANSI/NISO Z39.48-1992 (R1997). ⊛

Published with generous sponsorship from Wake Forest University Humanities Institute and the National Endowment for the Humanities
The National Endowment for the Humanities and the Wake Forest University Humanities Institute together: Democracy demands wisdom.

Designed by Hannah Gaskamp
Cover design by Hannah Gaskamp

Library of Congress Cataloging-in-Publication Data

Names: Erhardt, Marianne Jay, 1981– author. Title: Lucky Bodies: Essays / Marianne Jay Erhardt. Description: Lubbock: Texas Tech University Press, 2025. | Series: Iron Horse Prize | Summary: "A series of essays spanning the political to the personal, reckoning with motherhood and what counts as care"—Provided by publisher.
Identifiers: LCCN 2024057683 (print) | LCCN 2024057684 (ebook) |
ISBN 978-1-68283-252-3 (cloth) | ISBN 978-1-68283-253-0 (ebook)
Subjects: LCSH: Erhardt, Marianne Jay, 1981– | Mothers—United States—Biography. | Motherhood—United States. | LCGFT: Autobiographies. | Essays.
Classification: LCC CT275.E64 A3 2025 (print) | LCC CT275.E64 (ebook) |
DDC 973.934092 [B]—dc23/eng/20241211
LC record available at https://lccn.loc.gov/2024057683
LC ebook record available at https://lccn.loc.gov/2024057684

Printed in the United States of America
25 26 27 28 29 30 31 32 33 / 9 8 7 6 5 4 3 2 1

Texas Tech University Press
Box 41037
Lubbock, Texas 79409-1037 USA
800.832.4042
ttup@ttu.edu
www.ttupress.org

For my dad, Paul Joseph Upham, 1940–2022

CONTENTS

LUCKY
BODIES

YOU CALL
THAT WILD

For Max's mother in *Where the Wild Things Are* by
Maurice Sendak

The sailboats of imagination only float so far. When your
son Max settles into his, surrenders to the sea, in and out
of weeks, he is nowhere new. His boat is any boat. The sea
holds the usual salt. The Wild Things move with predictable limbs.
One has feet that are pale, hairless, human. Their teeth are terrible.
Their claws are terrible. The roars that they, well, roar, also terrible.
Their rumpus is nothing more than climb, carry, swing. You call that
Wild? I want to say. You call those Things?

As for Max, he is no Thing King. See the seams of his costume,
the thread of his storybook spine? Even when his walls dissolve into
branches and his bed is swallowed by vines, his wolf suit stays a suit.
As constant as the moon, the buttons row down his belly. He can
fasten them, but he wants you to. He won't tell you.

I think of my three-year-old boy at the college football game.
We sit on the crowded lawn, Nolan in my lap. His nails are already
bitten to the quick, but he is worried, giddy, and cuts crescent moons

into my arm nonetheless. This is how he takes the rush, impact, pom-poms, and ponytails. He swoons; he draws blood.

Later, at bath time, he tells me, *Mama. I am a costume. I am a mascot. I have someone inside of me.*

A wolf suit. A boy suit. The belly button memory of a mama tether. An odd stone to mark the buried time capsule of your before body. Did your husband wince when it was time to cut the cord? Did you do it yourself, scissors in your weak hand, slick with blood? Was it easy to split, to be so undone? When you shift now in the night, does your hand find your belly, that soft ridgeline from sternum to navel? Does it feel like quicksand, your mother costume, and does it suit you?

Milk ducts fill and drain. Hips widen beyond belief. We search for thick skeleton keys in our pockets but we have no pockets, and no treasure chests to worry open anyhow. We have breath grown loud as the shore. We have blue veins blooming, nonsense maps on the backs of our knees. In the water, relief. We are limber to the point of danger. Our new joints marry wonder and shame, thing and name.

Look. You made him that hairy costume. You hung his art at the bottom of the stairs. You are teaching him the distance between Max and By Max. Maybe not fast enough. Maybe too fast. He builds a fort. He nooses a stuffed bear. He cracks a wall. He runs with a fork, insatiable.

The youngest children learn things that fit in their mouths. This is why they try to grab the fat silver grape of the moon. This is why, by the sea, they keep licking the salt and sand from their fingers. And though they want their mothers whole, we only fit a bit at a time. And it hurts. When sleep is a lost runaway, when your nipples have turned to pulp and your baby shows no dissatisfaction with the taste of your blood in his mouth, you say, *He is killing me. Meal by meal, I am disappearing into him.*

Maybe this is why we are rarely named in children's stories. *Mother* is like mouth, leg, memory. A limb of the kid, pointless on its own. What name would you choose for yourself? Would you glue it on, belt it on, grow into it? Would you loop it on loose with a wild vine? See if it chokes? *Names are hard*, people would say to me during my pregnancies. What they meant was stories don't budge. Once told, just try and shake them off. My little Silas—*of the woods*—stares into storybooks. He is preoccupied with his inability to reach into a picture and pluck a person, dinosaur, strawberry, ocean from its pages. He worries for their freedom. *Stuck* he says. *Get them out.*

Silas is the one I call rascal, wild child, fearless. Not quite two, he climbs the tricky trees. Other mothers chide me at the park when they see him risk such heights. But even when he falls he is nimble. He floats, rolls, scurries off to some new exciting danger.

Nolan—*noble*—I tell my friends, is sweet, curious, cautious. He wants his feet on the ground. At the dinner table he stands on one leg, leaning on his chair. He won't go on a swing unless his feet can touch the mulch. As a baby, he refused to ride in a grocery cart or float in water. When we snuggle in bed, he presses the soles of his feet into my thigh. When he was a baby, it was my belly. But he has grown taller, and we line up differently now.

Why fixate on these stories, instead of others? Why not single out the times my grounded boy rises above it all? Why not describe Nolan as the boy who leaps between blue tiles at the grocery store? The boy who forgives too fast? And why not say how Silas announces he loves me, unsolicited, several times per day? Why not say that his body is brave but he worries, every time I put on the mask of my sunglasses, that I am leaving without him? That I am someone else?

When, friend, did you cave and bring Max his supper? Or had you planned to all along? Did you spend his punishment fretting, too lax or too stern? Did you skip supper yourself, go for a run, enjoy your own hunger, lick your lips as you zeroed in on the end of it, the relief there before you even got to the relief? Because the shout was out, the door was slammed; the two of you a pair. Wild insofar as wolves are wild. Still of this world.

We know wolves as villains. Tricking Little Red, donning Grandma's pajamas, huffing and puffing enough wind to knock down a dwelling. But their reputation is unfounded. Who doesn't long to roam and hunt? Who doesn't scale fences for livestock when their wild is abbreviated, their pack at stake? Who doesn't lie a little bit about who they are, to fit into or flee their family? Wolves, after all, raise humans as their own.

My mother's name is Janet—Jay—and she doesn't belong here. She says so herself one winter. I have traveled a thousand miles to visit, but there is no fanfare. We're not the kind to crown each other for showing up. We sit in the dining room, a high-ceilinged addition to our little ranch house, dreamed up by my mother and erected the summer I was born. I ask her to name her favorite room in the house, thinking we are in it. Without a blink, she answers, *the pink bathroom*. It's the warmest room in the house. The one with the lesser, dusty bathtub reserved for hanging wet bras and swimsuits. The closed hamper in front of the toilet, packed with forgotten dirty towels and topped with stacked Penny Savers and church bulletins. The countertop with a sprig of fake flowers that I assembled twenty years ago. The pink bathroom is her favorite, she says, but even so: *I've never really felt at home here.* I think she means the house, but she means all of it. *I'm really looking forward to the next life.* She looks up to Heaven. I look up, too. See the ceiling fan where a shredded Mylar balloon glinted for most of my childhood. *Cathedral*, Mom calls this ceiling. See the knots in the pine, shifting faces. Here and there, through the years, she floated the name *Great Room*, but it never took. Mom looks at me. She can't wait for this place to crumble.

Or: She splits like a mother has to split. Knows she is boat-bound and water-logged. Knows the daily disappearance. Knows that every wolf is also a pretend wolf, with gaps in the fur, failing seams where the sea air rushes in, finds tender skin.

And so, your son dreams up new walls and moons and bodies, ones he can already rule and abandon. For Max, there is only one Wild Thing that seems to trouble him. She is a sea creature, rising from under the surface, close to shore. In many ways, she's like all the others in the story. Muted colors, claws, terrible, terrible. But her lower body is a mystery, zipped up in the water. Max frowns, lifts his wolf paws to mirror the Thing. She could be kind. She could be killer. And she knows the way home.

THE BODY IS LOYAL

Choose someone to be the Mother.

~Rules to the game *Mother, May I?*

n one variation, the Children ask the Mother for permission to move their bodies in certain ways across the field. She's across the field, a figure turned away from them, gaze fixed on something in the trees. The Children are limber. The Mother, unpredictable. Sometimes she says yes. Other times, no. The Children play with the size of their requests. Two leaps forward? Five baby steps? One lamppost? *Yes, you may,* says the Mother. And the Children come to their knees, lie on their bellies, stretch their bodies as long as they will go. Where their fingertips reach—the buttercup, the acorn, the yellowing blade of late summer onion grass—this is where their feet are allowed when she gives them the signal to stand.

•

I am the Mother, almost the Mother, desperate in the belly of the night. These waves strike at one minute apart and last a minute each. No reprieve for twelve hours. I feel chased up a ladder, and the ladder is very tall, and the ladder is very loose, a set of stilts. I stand over my bed in the birthing center, fists in the mattress, moaning so forcefully that my voice is hoarse. Behind me, Maureen, the midwife, flanked by nurses. One places a white cotton washcloth, rolled up, between my teeth. *Bite this.* They promise that what is about to happen will be quick, but it will also amount to the most intense physical pain of my life. Far worse than the birth itself. Far worse than the ring of fire or the torn perineum I'll endure several hours from now. *Are you sure you want us to do this?* asks Maureen. I grunt my assent through the cotton, teeth tight. My tongue rubs the bumps of the cloth, exaggerated taste buds, no longer a cloth but another tongue I gnash with my molars. Maureen holds my hips, keeps my pelvis still as the nurses prep the four needles. In my periphery, I see each one widen her feet, find a soft plié, bracing for the peak of the next contraction. Maureen counts to three.

And they are exactly right. The pain is utterly blinding, the worst I have ever endured. I scream like a woman lost in time, like a woman biting a stick, a woman tortured, set to burn or left to drown, a woman whose scream will carry into the hall, the yard, the village, the future. It is one scream, and it ends. I let the damp towel fall from my mouth and crawl into the bed. I say *thank you.* I have manners.

The magic is in the pain, not the injection, which is only sterile water. It's a sleight-of-hand, a swap. To shock the nervous system, to disrupt its inventory of prolonged, relentless back labor, by flooding it with something worse. To force a mother's endorphins to rush, to drug her from within. To buy her some time before the transfer to the hospital. For a spell, the body and mind are mere neighbors. The pain gate between them can be open or closed. Or open but so overcrowded that it's rendered functionally padlocked, impossible for one version of pain to pass through.

•

The Winner is the Child who reaches the Mother first. The Winner touches the pattern of the Mother's sleeve and they swap roles. The Child figures out how to stand, where to look, now that she is the Mother. The tagged Mother, now a Child, runs back to the other Children, some of whom hold grudges about her earlier behavior. They suspect she had favorites. They feel she enjoyed her power too much. That she kept the Children in the sun too long. She stood too far away, remember that? And they could tell she was moving even farther away from them, taking baby steps she tried to mask with her long floral dress. The Winner vows to be different, to be her own kind of Mother.

There is no version of the game where the Mother is the Winner, although some Mothers will claim victory when they have been too cruel to let anyone get close and so the Children give up, or when the game runs out of time, when their own mothers call them inside for supper, noodles, and there is enough for everyone to have seconds but not thirds.

•

I am the Child. Not growing properly. I am naked from the waist up, humiliated, while the doctor and my mother discuss the flatness of my chest and the curve of my spine. I try to cover my chest with my wild hair, an appropriate mermaid who will never have to worry about never getting her period. But then I have to touch my toes, and so my hair sweeps the floor, and my doctor's hands are cold and clean and damp on my back. Seven degrees, she says. A touch of scoliosis. Something to keep an eye on. As I dress, I twist, try to see it. On the drive home, I accept that I am Judy Blume's *Deenie*. Who would have thought, of all the medical obsessions in my pre-teen books—leukemia, epilepsy, cystic fibrosis in several pink paperbacks—that I'd be a girl with a twisted spine. I make plans to hack off my hair, like Deenie does when she gets diagnosed. I find myself looking forward to a back brace, some surrogate body to inhabit. One afternoon, I pull on a green turtleneck, trapping my hair inside. I tug it loose a few inches, simulating how I'll look when I work up the nerve with the scissors. But the scissors never happen; the brace never happens. No mother, no doctor ever says scoliosis again. I don't cut my hair short for several years, and when I do, it is against my mother's wishes.

•

In another version, the Mother says yes every time. But don't mistake permission for generosity. The Children remain bound to her choreography. *Crabwalk back to Phillip*, she says, or *Do one cartwheel forward*. And it's not enough for the Children to simply obey. The Mother demands doubt, a double check, *Mother May I?* She'll say yes, but without fail, some Child forgets to ask, starts her cartwheel before Mother confirms her wishes, and the Child is sent all the way back to the starting line, which might be indicated by a pair of birch trees, a jump-rope stretched on the ground, a dropped cardigan, or, in my case, a stack of firewood where one evening I find a half-starved coyote poking around. She studies me, checks over her shoulder, looks at me again, then leaps over the barbed wire fence, into Henchion's pasture, where milk cows wander and nibble at grass.

•

I am the stack of firewood, the sack of bones, the undertrained dancer. I'm just a few years older than the undergraduates in this Advanced Modern workshop, but already I feel like their big awkward sister, their clumsy great aunt. It's a heavy-limb day, a body-is-a-chore day. With every movement phrase, I lose my breath overthinking my breath. Then we break into groups to observe and scribble notes on one another's improvisation. When it's my turn to move, I try to suspend my self-consciousness, adopt an agenda of authenticity, doomed to buckle. When I finish, the girl in the perfect messy braid says to her notebook, *You neglect your back body.* The other girls agree. In this moment, I feel both totally seen—*Yes, I do! I do neglect my back body!*—and utterly wounded. Neglect? That's the word to surface in the room when I move? For the remainder of the semester, I try to inflate the paper doll Marianne, to give her dimension. I close my eyes and awaken my trapezius, invite spaciousness into the links of my cervical spine. My ribs are not a ladder, or a line of piano keys. They wrap around me, hold me, contain me. I can send my breath between them and around them. I can let the breath go.

•

No, it's not the same basic game as *Simon Says* because Simon is nobody's Mother. Plus Simon talks about himself in the third person. Also, Simon faces you like a fool, no mystery, no chase. Simon only clocks your obedience. Mother measures your loyalty, your love.

•

I am the third person. The first person is the speech therapist who specializes in newborns. It's not that newborns should be speaking, but apparently eating is like speaking and this is where you go when the lactation consultant runs out of patience and the fenugreek has failed to up your milk production but has made your baby's urine smell like maple syrup in a bad way. The baby, Nolan, is the second person, though the therapist and I discuss him in the third person. She holds him, even though I am already holding him. I nurse him. She does not approve of the sounds he makes. They are the wrong sounds. She takes him in her arms and moves to different furniture. She offers him a bottle and he is happy to drink, doesn't care that she is not me. She wants me to watch. She says a lot of things but I only remember two. The first is that he won't be able to play contact sports. I should be skeptical or alarmed, but instead I feel impressed. She seems to know my baby much better than I do. She's some kind of wizard, predicting his future with a glimpse of his neck flexion. My neck works but my arms are empty. I begin to think that my arms will always be empty, that she will never give him back, that she is becoming his mother right in front of me. This possibility fills me with both dread and relief. If she walked out of this room with him, would I have the energy to follow? Would I be the mother who is devastated? Would I be the mother who takes a nap on a stranger's small office couch? The notion of sleep fills my chest with milk but I don't leak. I never leak, another way my body is wrong.

The second thing the therapist tells me is that I need to support Nolan's chin with every gulp he takes. When she says this she gives him back to me so I can prove I am capable. I hold a finger under his little jawbone and she teaches me how to push up into it, to encourage him to maintain suction. It is a dance, my hand, his chin, this rubber nipple. She says, *More pressure. You won't hurt him.* I don't believe her.

I stand to leave and I thank her for whatever this was. She says this was a consultation. That I should come back. That I should keep coming back and she will keep holding my baby and showing me things about his mouth. But I carry him away, away from the nap on the couch, through a doorway, away from smiling office manager, the fourth person. I don't stop at the checkout window, and the first and fourth persons are saying things back there but they don't chase me down. I am a lost cause. On the long drive home, foggy thoughts gather in my head, in my mouth, and I share them with Nolan. He coos and chirps, a string of perfect sounds.

•

Nobody wants to be It but everybody wants to be Mother. Except for the real mother. When she dreams up the game at a birthday party, she whispers it to a Child and takes no credit. She makes herself small and runs to the pack who will ask, *Mother May I?* She has no interest in standing alone far away, being pursued, granting permission and doling out punishment. Nevertheless, she has a long stride she fails to shorten. Before long, she outpaces all of the Children and nearly wins. When she tries to throw the game, omits the magic words, the Mother won't allow it. *You win, fair and square*, she is told. And because she failed to love their rules, the Children gang up on her or lose interest in the game, switch things up. They make her It. She has no say. She being It is all they want for the Child's birthday, for all of their birthdays, and she obliges. She chases them and does not catch them. She runs as fast as she can run. She follows them to their own front doors, which they slam. Under a streetlight, she shouts, *Olly Olly Oxen Free!* but by then the Children are dreaming.

•

Say you are the magic. Say you are the balm. Say you are the one they ask to map the field where mothers go. What on earth can you do with a lump in your breast or a shadow in your heart? What can you do when you are barely a wind-up toy needing a turn, when the knobs of your spine are impossible to grasp? One afternoon you are floating on your back in the Mediterranean. You are free. You are shining into the sea, into the sky, out your limbs and the tips of your hair, your crown. And you find you are too far from the shore to swim back. You are too tired. And there is no panic, just a pulse from somewhere. A whale, a star, a dead relative. Who can tell? You stay on your back, find a way to kick your legs so gently, barely, aiming your body for land, for your husband burning on the shore. The pulse might be your children, a decade away from arrival. And remember some summer in high school, running alone on the track at dusk. The sky too beautiful. The bounce of breath at the end of a sprint and some sudden grief, flooding love for your future children wrapped up in the love of your own child self. How you wept and wept and could explain it to no one. That you had met them on that field. That they came to you.

•

A bored Mother might be inclined to dare the Children. Steal, she might say, a healthy piece of bark from that maple tree. Chase the smallest Child until he falls. Count the sounds in the most forbidden word you know and walk that many steps forward, then say the word out loud that many times. Carry your supper into the woods and fall asleep with the bowl on your belly, noodles warm and fragrant. Last. At first light, emerge. Wash the bowl in the sink of any strange house. Find Mother, an early riser herself. She is tender in the morning. She will fill it.

•

Share, I say, *your weapons*. I don't call them guns because I don't allow guns. I do allow blasters, squirters, shooters, and Epic Battles. Gun, Gun, Gun, say my boys. No, a gun is never a toy, I say, filling a blaster with water. Even if it is pink plastic and every surface of the gun says Toy, Toy, Toy. Even if you are gifted one at your birthday party from the kindest child in the class, the child who tucks her trains into little beds at night, the child who will surrender the swing at the first hint of your want. Even then. Now, aim for the belly or the middle of the back.

I confuse them. One afternoon we walk home from the park and they find sticks of promising shape. They make shooting sounds, blast each other's white bodies, perform their wounds. They point their sticks at cars driving by and I grab the sticks. I shout. *Never! What if someone thought these were real guns? They would never think that*, they say. They can tell. My boys are comforting me, proof I am doing this wrong. *There are children*, I say. And somebody thinks they aren't playing. Somebody thinks they aren't children. Somebody has a real gun. Only I stop after *there are children. What children?* The boys want to know. I kiss them to fill the silence. The sky whitens, weighs its options. I fail, fall into my own imagined innocence. I change the shape of the story, pretend it's about permission. Tell myself this is age-appropriate. But for whom. Just. *You can play with*

*play guns. You already do. Call them guns. A blaster is a gun, a stick is a
gun, a pouch of candy is a gun full of rainbow-colored bullets.*

•

Of course, there are days when the Mother must be ready to catch
a raw egg in her hands. To cradle it in a spoon and run, run, run
without dropping it. Days the Mother shimmies into a real potato
sack—a couple of Yukon Golds forgotten in the corners—to hop
across the field. Some days the Mother's ankle tires of the twine that
ties her to the Father, ready for some race. She can be restless. In the
woods, I've heard, is the Grand Mother. And when you get to the
river, the Great Grand Mother. Great Great roams the mountain,
flies a kite along the ridgeline. Triple Great knows the valley, has
rested in every hollow. And so on.

•

At the base of my spine is a four-cornered diamond of bone, a dor-
mant kite. It's called the rhombus of Michaelis. It's where the needles go on that day I am almost a mother. They enter just shy of the
lateral corners known as the dimples of Venus. And while the circle
of the cervix is doing its magic, this wedge of bone is moving, too. It
floats up and out, bulging from my back, opening space in the pelvis.
Midwives say that, when the kite rises, the mother will raise her arms
above her head, instinct guiding her to hang on to anything to keep
her steady while whatever stability she has left in her pelvis falls away.
    It's good. It's supposed to fall away.
    When she reaches, the mother might find a bar above the bed,
hung for this purpose. She might find a door frame, a husband, an
exit sign, a tree limb, a lamppost. She might find there is nothing
to hold, not yet, but that her arms reach anyway, that the body is
loyal to more than itself.

•

ALICE IN OUTER SPACE

It's no use going back to yesterday because I was a different person then.

~Alice in *Alice's Adventures in Wonderland* by Lewis Carroll

My mother is afraid to fly, but she flies. To the Okinawa naval base to marry my father in 1965. From New York to Dallas for my brother's wedding, taking a separate flight from my father so that a fiery crash will kill only one of them. She flies to Florida in the weeks when her own father is dying. She flies to Paris, once, white-knuckles it over the ocean. But before all of that, she flies, in her head, all the way to outer space.

I find the story when Googling my mother. Who Googles their mother, when that mother is alive, just a two-hour drive away? When that mother was never not home to mother, save that trip to Paris, when we kids ran giddy with freedom? I Google her old name, her maiden name, eager for a glimpse of the girl she once was. Up comes the *1959 Waltham Mirror*, her high school yearbook, digitized by the Waltham Public Library. There are no pictures, and portions of the text are garbled. For Senior Superlatives, I can only guess what my mother won alongside Philip Conors. She did not win Personality Plus. She did not win Best Looking or Most Athletic. Most Likely to Succeed went to Robert Grady (Home Room Representative Alternate, Rifle Team) and Donna Carlstrom (Junior Red Cross, Honor SodetJ). My mother and Philip won MOST RI STC< TI.

Elsewhere in the yearbook, words work. She's described as *likable* and *one of Waltham's peppiest cheerleaders.* She was a go-getter, an award-winner, a Latin club and blood drive kind of girl. The kind who signed up for yearbook, this yearbook, where she was tasked with writing the Senior Class Prophecy.

Prophecy is a hefty term. Traditionally, these prophecies are a collection of simple one-liners. Predictions. *Maureen Forman will be an artist. Supriya Rao will win a Nobel Prize. Brian Hewson will be cast on* Survivor *and charm his way to victory.* I was on yearbook, too, but I don't recall what my classmates imagined for me, if they imagined anything.

My mother's prophecy went beyond a speculative attendance log of the graduates. Hers is a 2,300-word, ten-page story. Instead of isolated individual achievements, she imagines a city of graduates, overlapping futures, a world where all of her classmates continue to inhabit one another's lives. In her prophecy, kids grow up, but not away. Gerald Burke is on City Council. Millie Atkinson works in the newsroom. Dave Taranto runs a pizzeria. Joyce Doria is a comedienne. And when the protagonist, Alice, finds a ten-cent piece, she notes that it bears not the image of President Franklin D. Roosevelt but rather President Richard Hohman (Senior Play, German Club, Maroon Squad).

Alice, it is clear, is the stand-in for my mother, because while all of her classmates make a momentary appearance, Janet Yamartino doesn't exist in her own prophecy. There's only Alice. And who is Alice? What sort of future does my mother imagine for her near-self when she is 18, on the brink of life, her head full of stars?

A weary one.

Alice is a worn-out stay-at-home wife and mother. Her husband is a clumsy carpenter. Their teenaged daughter slogs through English homework while *viciously chewing her gum*. Alice notes that the book her daughter is reading *doesn't even have any pictures*. Alice, like my mother, dislikes books. Alice's young son, a real whiner, screams for milk and stories, neither of which the husband can provide because, when not tripping over things at Sawdust Carpenters Inc., he is consumed with his favorite television program, *The Quirk Quiz Show*.

Somebody taught my teenaged mother to abuse alliteration. Along with *Quirk Quiz*, we get a *luxurious limousine*, a *kumquat cannery*, and, early on, a *hysterical hare*. The hare? Yes. It's a Wonderland situation. Only this land is called Walthamland. Her city but not her city. And although the story is wholly hers to make, Alice's real adventures only happen in the prophecy's prolonged dream sequence. In my mother's wildest dreams, she can only dream.

My mother's Alice *dozes* off on the *divan*, stalks a rabbit, plummets down a hole, all of that. In Walthamland, she finds herself in that *luxurious limousine*, taking a tour of the lives of her classmates, whom, presumably, she has lost all contact with over the years though the rest have stayed in touch. She is an observer, an outsider, even when running into her old pals Helen LeBlanc (Glee Club) and Audrey Taylor (Senior Play Committee).

Alice wreaks havoc on her tour of Walthamland. It's a slapstick montage. First, a speeding ticket on Route 127. Then, while touring the local hospital, she's joyriding the state-of-the-art air-conditioned elevators, much to the chagrin of the staff who *hurriedly escort the visitors OUT*. Later, during a visit to the local television station, Alice's presence so disturbs a former classmate that she drops her microphone, trips over the wires, and falls flat on her face. The cameraman, Joseph Nason (Football, Baseball), pulls out his hair in distress. Alice, bewildered, makes a run for it, but not before interrupting a broadcast promoting the *cultural exchange of ideas for world harmony*. Alice enters the frame to add her two cents. The prophecy doesn't say what, exactly, Alice says on the subject of world harmony, only that, in the wake of her words, *Germany will probably never speak to the United States again.*

So Alice will speak her mind on television, but as for talking to her friends, it's not until she is strapped into a tourist rocket ship that she turns to them. And even then it's only for pleasantries. Soon she picks up a magazine to distract herself from her fear of flight. At liftoff, Alice cries out, to no one in particular, *Here we go!* with a *meek smile on her distraught visage.*

I have seen this meek smile. It's the one my mother puts on when she can't hear you but doesn't have the heart to tell you so. She has been hard of hearing for decades, eschews a hearing aid, and has all but given up trying to understand some of the staff at the assisted living facility, not to mention half of my siblings. And though I have been known to talk too fast or, God forbid, to mumble, she can usually understand me. I know how to enunciate. I know how to shout key phrases without sounding annoyed. It helps to think of her as very, very far away.

•

A few months prior to the print run of the *1959 Mirror*, the US launched the Pioneer 4 spacecraft from Cape Canaveral. Our answer to the Soviet Luna 1 two months prior, Pioneer 4 was the first American spacecraft to leave Earth's gravity. Its assignment? To photograph the surface of the moon, that daily but distant being. Unlike Pioneers 1 and 2, both failures, Pioneer 4 was *spin-stabilized*, meaning that it stayed true to course by spinning around its own axis. This rotation meant that small disturbances (thermal radiation, magnetic fields) wouldn't alter the trajectory. Such force would be tiny, negligible, when met with the established angular momentum. And indeed, Pioneer 4 managed to spin its way into heliocentric orbit. But, alas, it never took the pictures. We wouldn't get those until 1964 when Ranger 7 succeeded in capturing 4,300 lunar portraits. The phrase *lunar portraits* conjures, for me, an image of a moon seated on a wobbly metal stool, lit by fluorescent overhead lights, waiting for her school portrait. Maybe she's a senior and has been given a black shawl to wrap around her bare shoulders, to give the illusion of a gown. Maybe she holds a dirty plastic rose, handed off from moon to moon to moon through time.

After getting the photos, Ranger 7 crashed, scattering earthly debris across an area of the moon hence dubbed Mare Cognitum, or *Sea That Has Become Known*. In this case, knowing the sea means knowing that it's not a sea. That the early astronomers got it wrong. That this darker stretch on the moon holds no water, is only a basin formed by unfathomable, ancient impacts.

•

When it comes to prophecies, my mother prefers the Catholic variety. While she dislikes books as a rule, she does not shy away from the Book of Revelation. And unmoved by metaphor, she would no doubt register little surprise if she looked out her window tomorrow to see an actual lake of fire, patrolled by a leopard-like beast with the feet of a bear and the mouth of a lion. *Here we go!* she'd think. She'd be ready. I am one of seven siblings, with whom I shared a seemingly constant rotation of sacraments and sins. We knew very well that the Second Coming was, well, coming. And yet, as Megan O'Gieblyn notes in *Interior States*, this was *a kind of bone-marrow knowledge that the Lord is coming; that he has always been coming, which is the same as saying that he will never come; that each of us must find a way to live with this absence and our own, earthly limitations.*

Which is to say, we had to settle for lesser miracles. The weather, for one. How it could be promised, and then happen. My mother has always loved a cold front, a heat wave, a promise of a drop in pressure. Before my father died, and before she all but stopped going outdoors, not a day went by that my mother didn't ask him—the early riser, the paper-getter—*What's it like outside?*

There was also the lottery. Daily tickets, daily prayers. When leaving for an errand, my mother would routinely announce to any of us kids in earshot, *If I drop dead, the lottery tickets are in the top righthand drawer of my dresser.* If she died, she was saying, we should not assume ourselves unlucky.

For fun on a weekend afternoon, if my father wasn't using our sole television to watch VHS tapes of his mail-order *Victory at Sea* naval history series, my mother would indulge in documentaries tracing the Virgin Mary's visits to the modern world. The crying statues. The apparitions. The promises and predictions. She was a sucker for Fatima, where Our Lady promised to shake up the sky and, on October 13, 1917, made the sun dance for the tens of thousands of pilgrims who had gathered. The sun became a spinning disc, throwing off a cloak of storm clouds. It zigzagged and careened amidst plumes of smoke and bursts of color. It hurtled toward the earth, burning red, then retreated, fixing itself back into the sky like no big deal. The display that day was extravagant, but the message was not. Our Lady said to pray. And then to pray some more.

But maybe my mother's favorite Marian miracle was the Visible Host, which happened in her lifetime. July of 1962, Garabandal, Spain, the summer before she finished up her chemistry degree at Emmanuel College. There is video footage of the event. Calling for *a conversion of heart*, the Virgin Mary once again announced the miracle in advance, this time with a teaser: *The miracle will leave a permanent sign in Garabandal, which can be seen and photographed, but not touched.* On the appointed day, 13-year-old Conchita González stuck out her tongue for communion, which she claimed she had taken invisibly from Michael the Archangel several times before. This time, a perfect white disc appeared on her tongue, which she left hanging out of her mouth for a full two minutes, as if to say, *Take a good look, Doubting Thomases!* Then she swallowed it down.

My mother would tell us to *Look! Look!* at the grainy black and white footage playing on our 19-inch screen. But I couldn't discern anything extraordinary. A tongue, twitching with effort. A white circle or poor exposure. It would be the same when I was presented with ultrasound images of my own forming children. Their healthy, close-up hearts. I saw only moonscapes.

As for the host that appeared that day, one witness said, *It was white, but a white out of this world.*

•

When the rocket ship lands, intact, Alice is beside herself. *I want to put my feet on Saturna firma!* she says. This is vintage Janet. A desire for *terra firma* is something she expresses over and over, after a swim, a flight, a long drive, or even a sit on an oversized recliner. My mother never made it past five feet tall and, at 81, now stoops at a cool 4'7". It is not uncommon for her feet to dangle. I Google *Can you stand on Saturn* and find there is no real *Saturna firma* because the planet is a gas giant, with no surface at all, just a swirling of atmosphere with increasing pressure as you move in. In Alice's space-launch-within a dream–within a prophecy, however, Saturn is simply an extension of American suburbia, of Walthamland. Alice notes no otherworldly features here at all. Transplants live in Levittown, Saturn, and enjoy a university, bank, salon, and a watering hole called *Saturn Dry*. Alice's only moment of surprise comes when she sees an old friend, a former goody-goody. *She couldn't believe it; that is, she couldn't believe that Bob-ole-boy was smoking a pipe.* Janet Yamartino frowned upon smoking and drinking, whether it be done by men or caterpillars. She tried a gin and tonic once, but didn't like the way it made her feel. Out of orbit.

On Saturn, there are none of the awkward antics of Earthside Alice. She only marvels at how normal the planet seems, how undisturbed by her presence. Up here, there is abundance without chaos. Up here she notes the only color that appears in the entire prophecy.

The space money cradled in the bank vault, Alice delights to discover, is *of that glorious green hue*. It's not clear what shade of green is so glorious. Is it standard US currency, faded seaweed? Or is it some other, pulsing, alien chartreuse?

•

In Santa Mira greenhouses, bodies are coming to life. Santa Mira is the made-up California town in Don Siegel's 1956 *Invasion of the Body Snatchers*. The bodies, human on the surface, incubate in giant leafy seed pods until those pods ooze, open, and birth perfect replicas of Santa Mira residents, assuming their identities. The body snatchers will mow their lawns and wear their cardigans and pay their taxes. They'll do it all, in a dead-eyed manner, every human thing except for *love, desire, ambition, faith*, because, as one alien promises, *without them, life is so simple, believe me*.

But Miles and Becky, the couple on the run, don't want simple. Becky presses her face into Miles's chest, says, *I don't want a world without love or grief or beauty. I'd rather die*. Which, of course, she does. It's not apparent at first, but when Miles kisses her, Becky's lips are unresponsive, Becky's eyes are vacant. As promised, she's been *reborn into an untroubled world*, where, perhaps, there is no distinction between inner space and outer space.

Body Snatchers would have played at The Embassy, *Waltham's Wonder Theater*, when my mother was fifteen. When she was a different version of herself. Maybe a different self, one who had not yet become the wife and mother she imagined herself becoming. I wonder if she felt more alive then. If she felt less. I wonder if she was ever untroubled. Did a girl die? Did my mother hatch? In the film, pulp fiction comes from actual pulp. When the pods crack open, the sound effects are made by men holding vegetables in their hands, holding and crushing those vegetables—eggplants, peppers, yellow squash, right up next to microphones.

Miles tries to warn his neighbors, but almost nobody in Santa Mira believes him. Shout, *I'm not crazy!* and you're bound to be deemed crazy. Miles is met with a white coat, a head doctor, whose clinical opinion is that Miles is *madder than a March Hare.*

•

When my son is five I take him to see a production of *Alice in Wonderland*. He crushes on the caterpillar, his babysitter. He is entranced with the scenes where Alice changes size. When she is tiny, the set pieces are enormous, the rocking chair much too large for her to climb into. When she grows, off in the wings, stagehands fit her body into a cardboard house. Her arms emerge out the windows, her chin rests on the roof. My son leans in and whispers, *It's called Wonderland because people go there to wonder.* Indeed. *Why is a raven like a writing desk?*

When I was a child, I performed in a low-budget community production called *Alison Wonderland.* I appeared in one scene, where the playing cards anxiously paint the roses red. I was the roses—green leotard and tights, with dozens of red tissue paper flowers pinned in place all over my body. On my head, felted leaves and another enormous flower. My job was to dance while being painted. My job was to be a girl impersonating a rosebush impersonating a red rosebush. I did it well. The following Halloween, my mother dug the costume out of the hamper and made me wear it. She had spent ages on it, after all. It was her prerogative. But the tissue paper flowers were terribly flattened. And without the story around me, nobody could understand what I was. They guessed elf, clown, the wrong kind of plant. *Yes,* I said, to every parent in every doorway, *that's me.*

•

Alice's visit to Saturn is brief, only one out of the ten pages of the Prophecy. She takes space money as a souvenir and returns to the rocket, now Earthbound, *with the speed of light, in a cloud of dust, and a hearty Hi-ho processed aluminum*!

What my mother couldn't foresee in 1959 was that, fifty years later, a new aluminum concoction would emerge: Aluminum-Ice Rocket Propellant, or ALICE. An environmentally friendly replacement fuel, ALICE powered its first small rocket in 2009. Also of note, ALICE could, theoretically, be manufactured in outer space, with raw materials found on the moon and other celestial bodies. ALICE could be from anywhere.

Whoosh!!! "Back to Earth already?" our little darling asked. That they were, and a big surprise was awaiting Alice.

•

Leaving a planet changes a person. Astronauts have been known to experience the *overview effect*. To be awestruck into a lasting cognitive reorientation. Person. Planet. Rotation. Aliveness. Vast bodies turn tiny. Tiny bodies turn vast.

When my mother was pregnant with her first child, my eldest sister, she was also dying. And she did die, briefly, in a white room at Mass General. She remembers floating above her body, looking at herself from above with only mild curiosity. She remembers thinking, *Well, somebody else is going to have to raise that baby,* as if the baby would somehow survive if the mothership did not.

Two years later, not dying, she would give birth to her second child, a boy, and two months after that Apollo 11 would float itself down onto the surface of the moon. The babies would hardly remember, but my mother would keep a pristine copy of the *Time* magazine from July 25, 1969, which she would later give to my son, a kid she might describe, as she once described me with varying levels of affection and accusation, as a *space cadet*, with his *head in the clouds*. Much of the issue is devoted to the moon landing, although before you get to the moon you find a full-page advertisement for sugar. The ad shows a Mary Tyler Moore replica (or perhaps it is actually Mary Tyler Moore), seated at a lunch counter with a sandwich and a bowl of soup. She is, apparently, *over-hungry*. No woman should crave so much. Sugar, the ad promises, is the answer to that sense of lack, that *fat time of day*, when you're *ready to eat two of everything*. Sugar will *fill that hollow feeling*.

A few pages later, men walk on the moon, satisfied. *Time* shares Neil Armstrong's famous *giant leap* line, getting it wrong. *Time* quotes him as saying, *That's one small step for man*, but Armstrong insists that his words were, *That's one small step for* a *man*, going so far as to annotate the NASA transcript himself. But the *a* is not audible. Even Armstrong admits, when he listens to the recording, that he hears no *a*. It's not until 2006 that *a computer analysis of sound waves found evidence that Armstrong said what he said he said*.

Time also reports that, while Armstrong studied the lunar land-scape, his wife, another Janet, studied him on the television, calling out, *Be descriptive now, Neil!*

And he was. *It looks like a collection of just about every variety of shape*, he says. *Angularities, granularities, every variety of rock you could find.* He notes *a stark beauty all its own. It's like much of the high desert of the United States. It's different, but it's very pretty out here.* Studying the moon dust on his boots, he reports, *It does adhere in fine layers, like powdered charcoal, to the sole.*

Those dirty boots, I read, do not come home. The astronauts leave behind any equipment not necessary for the trip back, including boots and backpacks. They also leave behind an American flag, embellished with wire so as to give it the appearance of blowing in the wind. But there is no wind on the moon.

•

When the rocket lands back in Walthamland, Alice is immediately whisked away to a party in her honor. She assumes it is a birth-day party. *It wasn't her birthday, but she didn't want to say anything that might cause a riot.* This is Earth, after all, the place she caused all that trouble. But there are no birthday (or unbirthday) rituals. The Prophecy never says what the party is for, or why Alice is the guest of honor. Met by Walthamland Goodwill Ambassadors, she enjoys *Fay's Finest Fruit Juice* and *Baldaro Loaf Bread smothered with Olofson Oleo.* There are speeches, celebrities. Everyone is a graduate. My mother writes, *Everything was utterly wonderful, classmate after classmate chatting and chuckling with Alice.*

When I read this Prophecy, I recall two moments in my mother's life. The first happened when she was a teenager. Her mother, a chronically depressed and aloof, bookish woman, stood at the kitchen sink, washing fruit or cleaning a dish or simply letting the water run over her hands, as my mother sometimes does. As I sometimes do. Outside, she saw a light.

I'm getting this wrong. My mother tells me that her mother was in bed. But in my head my grandmother is always at the sink, an apparition turned away from me. A face I never saw up close, as she died before I was born. A face I'll never see.

My grandmother saw the light, saw the oval-shaped ship in the sky. She felt no fear, only awe. My mother says, *I assume she was awake.* When I ask if she believed her, my mother says *yes.* My grandmother was *not the type to tell tall tales.*

By January of 1959, yearbook underway, my mother was still wondering about UFOs. She wrote to the U.S. Air Force for information and received a reply dated January 19th, signed by M. K. Marsh CBO (W-3), WSAF, Directorate of Administrative Services. Marsh thanks her for her interest and suggests she visit her local library to find books titled *The Report on UFO, Flying Saucers from Outer Space,* and *Flying Saucers Conspiracy.* I Google these titles and find that all three attest to a Pentagon cover-up, that they swear to the existence of aliens. Also, these books have pictures.

The second moment that comes to mind happened during a conversation I had with my mother when I was home on break from college. She told me that, as an ardent Catholic, she was *really looking forward to the next life.* And while some of that had to do with wanting to bask in the presence of her dead loved ones as well as her Lord and Savior Jesus Christ (although truth be told, she was more pumped to meet Our Lady, every Catholic's one, true Mother), she seemed mostly excited for how welcome and comfortable she imagined she would feel in Heaven, admitting, of Earth, *I never really felt at home here.*

All of which is to say, when I read this Prophecy, where my mother unbuckles herself from a spaceship and is somehow made whole through reunion, I think of her own chronic depression. The way she stared out the window. The anxious nights where she found no rest. The rage that came and left us wondering, *Where on Earth did that come from?* I think of the unfathomable distance between some children and mothers. And I can only assume that Janet Yamartino, even in her cheerleader days, even when she started The Sunnytones singing group with Theresa and Audrey and Helen, even when she won the DAR Award and did the Christmas Show and volunteered as an Open House Usher, that she wondered, in her still hatching heart, if she was some kind of alien.

.

When Armstrong and Aldrin return from the moon, they go into a gleaming quarantine facility for 21 days. Scientists study, measure, wait to see if some lunar microbe, some tiny secret seed, will kill them all, will alter Earth forever. But no seeds take hold. No pods enclose them, replace them.

Alice gets no such chance to reacclimate. Instead, she is jostled out of the Walthamland dream by her husband, Peter, who asks if she was having a nightmare. *No,* she says. *I was just dreaming.* Peter is waking her because their son is calling out upstairs, and Peter is too busy watching his precious *Quirk Quiz Show* to assist.

Cue my father, watching *Jeopardy.* Cue my gaggle of siblings, needing and needing and needing. Once, I remember I was little,

I snuggled up against my mother on the old plaid couch. Or I tried to snuggle up to my mother. She pushed me away. She said it was too hot. Maybe it was. Maybe she snuggled me a thousand other times and I simply have no memory of it. Maybe she was simply, in that moment, bodied out, as I have felt with only two children to her seven. Maybe I didn't even want to snuggle, was just trying to become another version of myself, a daughter in a story who was drawn to the mother right in front of her. I don't remember trying ever again.

The little boy is still calling out and Alice, half-awake, lumbers up the stairs, carrying a bottle of Dougan Dairy milk (Maureen Dougan: Glee Club, Prom Committee). But the boy rejects it. Alice is always offering her child the wrong things. *I don't want my Dougan Dairy milk!* he screams. *I want you to read the story of Alice in Wonderland to me!*

Alice does what any star in any story set in space must do. She feels the pressure, the heat, the center of gravity, heavy on the horizon. The child wants a story. The mother knows the story. But, for a glittering constellation of reasons, she cannot bear to tell it. Alice empties herself of love, desire, ambition, and faith. She turns vegetal. The final sentence of the prophecy is only two words. *Alice collapsed.*

•

In 1967, the United Nations put forth the Outer Space Treaty, declaring the Moon, Saturn, and all celestial bodies as *the province of all mankind.* No one can claim Outer Space, though some have tried. Two years after the treaty, Bishop William Donald Borders of Orlando declared himself the first Bishop of the Moon, pointing to the Church's 1917 Code of Canon Law which declares that *any newly discovered territory fell under jurisdiction of the diocese whence the expedition left.* Apollo 11 left from Cape Canaveral. The local diocese has maintained a Moon Bishop ever since.

In 2008, Jesuit Father José Funes, director of the Vatican Observatory, speculated on the existence of aliens and to what extent they might be a part of mankind. Funes sees aliens as totally compatible with the teachings of Catholicism, and says that, if they exist, they are our *extraterrestrial brothers*. At the same time, he says, we should not assume that our sins are theirs. *God became man in Jesus in order to save us. So if there are also other intelligent beings, it's not a given that they need redemption. They might have remained in full friendship with their creator.*

Aliens didn't ruin the garden. Maybe they have no knowledge of gardens, no need. Maybe they are their own gardens—green and entangled and abundantly alive, full of nourishment we have yet to comprehend. It is possible they have no need for our understanding, or for our forgiveness.

In 2021, the University of Arizona's SpaceTREx laboratory announced new research towards building a Lunar Ark, that is, a biodiversity storage hub on the moon. The Lunar Ark would back up 6.7 billion species of life from Earth: seeds, spores, sperm, eggs, fungi. In case all of Earth needs to be reborn, forgiven.

•

In the fall of 1980, my mother is newly pregnant with me when the Voyager 1 flies by Saturn, sending images back to Earth. The planet's rings, once thought to consist of *bland, featureless sheets of material separated by gaps* turn out to resemble *grooves on a phonograph record,* a series of *braided features and spiral structures* shaped by small moons—moonlets—in and around the rings. Also, *patterns that looked like propeller wings spiraling out.* Also, the rings are made of ice. And maybe rock, old moons, space junk.

In addition to collecting what truth it can, Voyager 1 carries on board a gold-plated copper Golden Record sealed in aluminum, an offering to any and all intelligent life it might encounter on its journey. The record keeps an image of a baby in utero. Keeps the *Life* magazine cover with gymnast Cathy Rigby on the beam. Keeps *Beethoven's 5th*, and Blind Willie Johnson's *Dark Was the Night*.

Voyager, which traversed the end of the heliosphere in 2012, now soars through interstellar space. NASA expects to retain contact into 2025, although in 2023, Voyager 1 began transmitting *gibberish* to NASA. Meanwhile its companion, Voyager 2, fell silent for a few weeks when its antennae got pointed in the wrong direction. Away from us. For now, both continue to soar.

Voyager's follow-up, Cassini, had no such luck. Cassini, which taught us more about the moons of Saturn, the methane lakes of Titan and geysers of liquid water bursting from Enceladus, got only 20 years. Sent us over 400,000 images. Began running short on fuel, not an ideal situation for a vessel packed with pods of plutonium-238, a *nuclear heart*. Concerned that Cassini might crash into one of the moonlets, which hold the potential to support life, NASA decided to hasten and aim the ship's death spiral. On September 15, 2017, my mother's 76th birthday, Cassini was steered straight into Saturn's upper atmosphere, where it melted and possibly exploded.

Of the crash, one NASA thermal engineer said, *It would be a tremendous view, if anyone could witness it.*

My mother's heart would crash soon after. It began with a narrowing, poor oxygen. It left her dozing through the day from the lack. They replaced one of her valves with a valve from a pig. We don't need humans for that anymore. And that was supposed to be it. But then, chaos. Her blood pressure plummeted to 45/30. I wasn't there. I was driving across the state to catch my final glimpse.

Somehow, my mother was able to talk. With a BP that low, she shouldn't have been talking. It was a miracle she was talking. Her voice was garbled, as the hollow of her chest cavity filled with her own blood. What she said was, *I do not consent.* To the surgery. To the broken heart. To all of the impacts she'd endured in 81 years, so many unknown to me.

The doctors saved her anyway. Cracked her open. Declared her *good as new.* Propped her up in a chair to begin recovery. She wasn't allowed to raise her arms so we fed her whatever she wanted. Coffee, which she never cared for before. A spoonful of vanilla ice cream, which she held on her tongue to savor. If she wasn't wearing an ugly green gown, with all those tubes reaching out like tentacles, and if there wasn't so much old blood and gauze and doubt and loneliness every time we turned around, we might have mistaken her for royalty. This was no Alice. This was Janet, Queen of our Hearts.

HOT TICKET

for Aunt Joan

n exchange for a dying newborn sister, my mother gets naming rights. Janet names you Joan, holds you Joan. She is eight years old. Yours is an unremarkable death, in a time where a baby too early, too small, goes fast. Demands no tiny coffin or ceremony. Just one of those things.

In my dreams, you live. Janet gives you the bottle, knows her way around diaper pins. She teaches you to clap, to tie your shoes with bunny ears. Calls you Joanie. Jo. Bunny-boo. Sissy. You are the wild one, the bold one. You are a beauty, but not the beauty. You and Jay are a rare pair, a team. She is petite, curvy. She has the dark hair cut to the chin, sunglasses, sparkle smile. She is tap shoes, impeccable rhythm, and secrets. You are lighter, longer. Your limbs, your hair, your laugh. Everything about you extends. You hold nothing back. Some would call you a loose woman, but my mother, who is at times maddeningly moralistic, forgives your gregariousness, the way she does her father's cigarettes, her brother's blunt. *You are a hot ticket.* Jay tells you this, again and again. It is the greatest compliment she bestows on anyone, ever, and she gives it to you.

You never have children, you never want them all to yourself. But your love is fierce and never fleeting. You, our favorite aunt.

You travel, but not for long. You bring us treasures, but nothing that we have to treat tenderly. Rocks from the West Coast. Wedges of a decadent cake you make on a whim after finding the recipe in a lady's magazine in a doctor's waiting room. You bring us corn to shuck in the summer. At Christmas, we open boxes of old keys, a leather pouch full of thimbles, a pair of roller skates to share. *Take turns*, you say, like it's no big deal and like magic we are generous with one another. Like magic the skates fit all of us. You have a pink silk dress you wear to parties. In the hem, you've sewn a handful of tiny bells. When you move across the room, you are an angel, a gift shop door. Heads turn.

They find the tumor in your breast, take it. You joke that losing a breast is no big deal because you never had much to begin with. *Better me than you*, you say to Mom. *Not now, Joanie*. It is not the time to joke, or to die, and you don't. Because that is the other thing. Death never catches up with you. *Joanie is invincible*, we say about the cancer, the time you almost drown, the time your bus catches fire in South America.

And Jay isn't reading your postcards with jealousy. Jay is not despondent on the couch, while her seven kids destroy the wood floors. We don't drink a gallon of milk in ten minutes. We don't demand to be carried, or to walk across the street with our hands free of hers. If we do it is forgivable, because you, dear, never leave her out. You're picking her up for drinks later. You're calling from a stint in Chicago, eager to gossip. On a whim, you're on your way home. You're stopping over to drop off a lottery ticket and fold the warm laundry with her. Next weekend, the Yamartino sisters are taking Metro North down to the city to see a show. *Here's a new lipstick, Jay*, you say. My mother wears lipstick when you give it to her.

Joan, my mother never said to me, as I bickered with my four sisters, pulling hair, doling out humiliation, she never said, *You are lucky to have a sister!* I didn't even know you'd existed until I was a teenager. She'd had a miscarriage, said, *God takes care of these things*. She said your name then.

You took care of her. Taught her how to love women, love being a woman. Her mother, your mother, read books and cried. *That's all she did*, Mom snaps at me one afternoon when I am nose-in-the-V of another novel. But you never read. You never cried.

There were no other sisters. A shame since I had sisters to share. One who almost burned the house down boiling bottle nipples, left us standing in the yard while the smoke settled. One who nearly met a bullet meant for a deer. One who got so thin she could slip between piano keys. One who charmed us all, dreamed up imaginary friends when we weren't enough, grew her hair practically to the floor. We weren't as good as you, but we were sisters.

But Jay couldn't have us. She was stuck with us as daughters. She gave us the names that were unsuitable for you. She didn't braid our hair. She would have braided yours. She didn't lie in bed with us. She didn't tell us her secrets. We didn't tell her ours.

This summer, at the beach, we are all together. And Mom makes it to the water's edge one day, complaining that it's *a production*, using two golf clubs as improvised canes (because, Joan, she refuses a cane. Only you could convince her otherwise). The image of your name, in Grandpa's cursive, folded up in a Bible, rises in my mind. I ask where you are. Mom remembers no burial. No church pews or held hands or songs sung. No dirt. No darkness. She is uninterested in these facts. What she wants to tell me about is your name, borrowed from Joan Holloway, who I know as a fictional character on a throwback TV drama. But the real Joan Holloway was a tap dancer tapping when tap was dying. She didn't make it far. One appearance on *Ed Sullivan* and a few stints on a variety show called *Toast of the Town*. Mom's eyes sparkle when she remembers Joan Holloway. I find footage of her later. She looks just like you. At a brief close-up, I see she also looks like Grandma Mary, only not reading, not crying. Her movement is Trisha Brown in the arms, Judy Garland in the shoes. Fluid but spunky. She wears a long skirt and a loose satin shrug that makes her look like a girl with half-grown wings. She's all limbs and rapid taps. So fast she seems to barely keep up with her own feet as they cross the stage. She vocalizes, nonsense. She cups her hands around her mouth as if she is about to say something you might understand, but it's just a breath, she's out of breath, and then a little wail. She is amazing or she is ordinary; we will never really know. Her routine ends with a series of long-legged pirouettes. The kind that dazzled us when you took us all to *The Ice Capades* one winter. I count at least twenty-two rotations. She makes them look easy in a way that might leave an audience wondering if she lacks true talent. But they love her anyway. They love her enough. Because look at her go. And go. And go.

BIG TIME

80% of sightings go unreported.
                              ~The Bigfoot Field Researchers Organization

t's almost Christmas, December 21, 1972. Ten minutes up the road from my parents, deep in the woods, a blast. The flame is orange. The smoke is black. The roof of an unassuming concrete building lifts up, then drops. A set of steel doors is knocked off its hinges. A man's watch melts clear to the bone of his wrist. The blaze is brief. Here, then gone. Then sediment coats the bare tree branches, the handful of vehicles in the gravel lot. It scatters across the quiet lake like snow. And then there is actual snow coming down. Just a bit, mixed with rain, mixed with the dust. It won't be a white Christmas, too warm this year for snow to stick. The lake hasn't frozen yet; it drinks in everything that falls from the sky. Left behind, after the ambulance races off to Vassar, is the man's vomit, two shattered windows, what's left of a concrete wall. Also, weapons-grade plutonium.

The holiday will come and go before locals read the story in the *Chronicle*. A week will pass during which they will wear their new slippers, polish off the tiny chocolate Santas softening in the toes of their stockings hung by the hearth. My mother will fill the spaghetti pot with water from the tap and leave it on the stovetop overnight. She does this often in the winter since winter means weather and weather means we could lose the power to our well's electric pump. She has three children so far. Her goal is six. I'll be number six. She'll get lucky, get to seven, despite a scatter of miscarriages. When her children are grown, the lining of her uterus will fill with a rare cancer. She'll call it *a slap in the face*. A different kind of cancer, okay, but this? After all of those pregnancies, babies, teenagers? Her womb, a slapped face.

A week for the news to break. Three years for the facility cleanup. Trucks haul poisoned soil. Geiger counters aim here, then here. The site is declared *safe* although a radioactive hotspot is found more than a decade later, after United Nuclear Corporation has shut down the site and sold the land and the lake to the National Park Service. I am five when they reroute the Appalachian Trail to take advantage of the acquisition. Turns out that an oasis optimal for secret experiments is also ideal for a nature retreat. Soon, thru-hikers swim in the water, hang hammocks from the leafy oaks. They name themselves Panther. Promise. Roam. Tortuga. They filter the lake water with hand pumps and drink it down. Years later, I picnic there. It's the summer I am trying to get pregnant. My friends and husband swim. I am in my suit, hot, but I don't. A whole life can be mapped around the moments one refuses to get in the water. My hand on my belly, the sheen of Lycra. A strawberry in my mouth. A stitch of worry, but at twenty-nine, I've never even heard about the blast, just some rumors that the lake is tainted or haunted. Nuclear Lake has something to do with nuclear.

Some stories:
- The lake is crystal clear, perfect.
- The lake is crystal clear, nothing alive inside.
- Buried in the lake are barrels, were barrels until they disappeared.
- Buried in the lake is a Jeep, which someone tried to drive across the ice one winter.

- Buried in the lake are forty-one mysterious metal objects, demanding further investigation.
- Moving in the lake are twelve-inch sunnies and giant bass, the size of crocodiles. Their teeth tear through fishing line. It's the best spot in town to fish. But don't eat the fish.
- At night, the water glows. It's beautiful.
- At night, moving in the woods, is a family of Sasquatch. Their tracks can be found heading into the water. Or away from the water.

It is this last promise that brings the TV cameras to Pawling the following December. *Finding Bigfoot* is an Animal Planet series. It's everything I imagine it will be. Blurry dramatizations. Aerial shots of Hudson River bridges, heavy forest. Weatherman conspiracy voices. They say my town is a *Quaker village*. Yes, the town was founded by Quakers but the only meeting house is The Meeting House, a restaurant on Route 22 where high school theater friends and I would order mozzarella sticks and Cokes after dress rehearsals for *Brigadoon*. We felt appropriate in our comfy clothes, our stage makeup and hard hairdos. We felt not unlike the middle-aged townies we dreaded becoming. They reeked of Marlboros and Aqua Net. They drank until they were barely bipedal. Until they were stupid. Happy. Maybe this is what the TV men mean when they say that we *live rurally*. Still, plenty of folks in my Podunk town hop on the Metro-North to Manhattan every weekday at dawn, shirts pressed.

The lead host of *Finding Bigfoot* is Matt Moneymaker, yes really, founder and president of the Bigfoot Field Researchers Organization. Moneymaker notes a cluster of sightings around the Appalachian Trial, including Nuclear Lake. He makes no mention of, likely has no knowledge of, the explosion, the radiation, the possible half-life danger lurking. Only the bipeds in the shadows, the Bigfoot, who rattle tents, who scream in the darkness, but who wish us no harm.

Moneymaker takes particular interest in a Bigfoot encounter detailed by Robert Boyd, who shares his story at a town hall meeting that does not appear to be held at the town hall. Is it the Book Cove? The historical society? Someone's large, empty storefront? Robert says that he and his girlfriend were camping when they heard heavy, deliberate footsteps, when a creature messed with their tent. Robert never saw the animal, which proves to be one of the strongest pieces of evidence for a bona fide Bigfoot encounter. Moneymaker's co-host declares, *Even you not seeing one points to a Sasquatch encounter because most of the time people don't see them.* The Bigfoot Field Researchers Organization website claims that 80 percent of sightings go unreported because people fear ridicule. Finding Bigfoot spans one hundred episodes. And that's merely a fraction of the believers. Sasquatches are everywhere.

Bobby Greffrath, another town hall witness, agrees. Bobby wears a chin line beard and plaid shirt and claims to have seen Bigfoot at the West Dover Road AT access, the same place where my husband parked his Chevy Corsica, white with red interior, on our first date, a hike to the Cat Rocks. It was March of '99. We were seventeen. We tromped through what was left of the winter snow. Rob said the crunching sound reminded him of someone eating cereal, and I relished being with a boy who noticed when things sounded like other things. He held my hand. We didn't see any Bigfoot that afternoon. We didn't kiss. What Bobby Greffrath saw was a Squatch grabbing a grocery bag that had been left on the side of the road. The *black, hairy mass* was hungry and disappeared behind the Dover Oak, supposedly the largest tree on all 2,200 miles of the Appalachian Trail, a monster of a tree, over 20 feet in diameter. The grocery bag, anyone could see, must have been a food drop for a hiker. Hasn't Bobby Greffrath ever seen how hairy these hikers can be? How their packs enlarge them? What's in the bag? Lipton noodles. Peanut butter, A block of cheese. Maybe some fresh fruit, a luxury, to be eaten right away. Peels and pits tossed into the woods.

Bobby Greffrath, like my town, knows a thing or two about monsters, for Bobby Greffrath is an actor. Does he list *Finding Bigfoot* on his resume? Does he wear plaid in his headshot? In regional theater productions, he plays Jekyll and Hyde's best friend Utterson. Then the sadistic dentist in *Little Shop of Horrors*. He shines as Frankenstein in Rhinebeck. No lines, but the audience loves his grimaces and grunts.

What does a Bigfoot sound like? That depends. Are we talking vocalizations or wood knocks? Male or female? Adult or juvenile? On the hunt or mourning their dead? Listen. They sound like whatever sounds are out there. Yowling. Howling. A snapped branch. A scream. *The New York Times* describes Moneymaker's simulated call as *a cross between a police siren and an ill baby*. But there's also silence, another way they stay hidden when huge.

In footage featured in the Pawling episode, no one hears a baby Sasquatch swinging in the trees at Lembo Lake. It's a home video taken at a music festival campground. The people are drunk or high. They howl, *Act natural!* and laugh at the fire, where food heats in a can. The camera captures the pond's perimeter, studded with fires like theirs, with song. In the background, the baby unsub (short for *unidentified subject* on the Sasquatch chat rooms) leaps off the shoulder of an adult unsub, then swings from tree branches *It's a gibbon*, says the show's resident skeptic, field biologist Ranae Holland. But researchers have checked with surrounding animal facilities, and no gibbons have gone missing. No pets were allowed at the festival. And who lets their gibbon play in a tree? How good are gibbons at coming back when called? And Holland wants to believe, at least a little. In a later episode, she leaves an actual gibbon caged on a hillside, hoping to lure her primate cousins. In another, she sets a boom box out in the middle of the night, plays a recording of a crying human baby. Perhaps this will draw out a Squatch, who must be curious. Who must be wired to care for babies. *I just want something to happen, that's all. Something definitive,* Holland says. But the night yields little. There's eye shine in the brush, but it belongs to a deer. Squatch food, sure, but not a Squatch. Is there no mother in these woods? No nursing Bigfoot whose chest dampens with milk when she hears the recording? Who would risk being seen, being heard, even captured, to tend to such a vulnerable creature?

2017. Another film crew sets up shop in Pawling. It's big time. Actress Emily Blunt straps on a fake belly. Her husband, John Krasinski, grows an impressively full beard. He's picked Pawling to shoot *A Quiet Place.* This time, the monsters aren't half as hairy as he is. They are futuristic, armored, enormous. They walk on all fours. They would swoop right in if they heard the baby tape. Blind, sound is how they find their kill. So, the family drags a mattress across the trap door to a basement bunker. They play Monopoly with pieces of felt. They plate soft dinners onto verdant leaves of Swiss chard. They scatter sand on the paths they will walk. They know which steps creak and where.

We're supposed to think, *Oh shit.* How is Emily Blunt going to have a baby in silence? Won't she have to moan, to call out, to bang shit around? And what about the baby? How can you explain to a baby that it just needs to forget its vocal cords? We're supposed to forget our popcorn, to whisper to one another about the errant nail on the basement steps, the light-up toy in the hands of the foolish boy, bound to sing. We're calibrated for fear, but when Rob and I watch the film at my sister's house in Buffalo one winter, it feels cozy. The danger is so complete that it suffocates, soothes. As parents of two small and noisy children, we romanticize the life of the little nuclear family on the screen, living where we might have if we had stayed, right there at the barn at Lakeside Park, where I taught summer camp drama to children flexing their outside voices, where Rob and I watched the sunrise after prom and laughed out loud. In the film, the family lives in a hush. They never grow tired of the sound of their own names. Emily Blunt might hear *Mom* only every few weeks, when they traipse to Buttermilk Falls. There, the family can duck under the precipice, hide behind the sound of the spill. They can speak freely, shout if they feel like it. Water absorbs every word. When Krasinski dies, we relax even more. Glad that his scream was brief. Glad that we can go back to hearing the rustle of our clothing, the wind building outside, lake effect snow not far off. No worries. We're tucked in here. This old house has good bones and a humming furnace. My brother-in-law closes the front curtains, and, as he does every night, calls out, *Show's over, perverts!* to anyone who might be lurking, tempted to stare, to make up a story.

What's the half-life of a legend? Fourteen years after the nuclear explosion, the injured technician, long quiet, makes a surprise visit to a meeting of the Nuclear Lake Management Committee. His name: Kevork Parseghian. Sworn to secrecy after the accident, and scared of going the way of Karen Silkwood (who died in a mysterious 1974 car accident en route to share her nuclear contamination story with *The New York Times*), Parseghian has been living in California. Why does he surface now? Because the reports are wrong. Because United Nuclear Corporation no longer exists, and the risk of making some noise is dissipating. Because he happens to be in town, visiting his father.

Parseghian makes no mention of time stopping, no watch melting when the lab burns. In fact, time moves with deliberate footsteps. The day of the blast, his hands are in the *glove box*, a contraption that allows him to shape radioactive material with gloved hands inserted into two ports. The box looks like an incubator for a premature baby. It's supposed to be filled with helium or nitrogen, but cost-cutting measures have run them out of gas. *All the dials were zero,* says Parseghian. And zero means there's oxygen—the wrong air—in there. Oxygen means volatile. Only five minutes until his break time. He's about to take two weeks of vacation. He polishes a final pellet, notes a stubborn bump, flips on the grinder. And.

When he comes to, it's to heat. Glass in his face, a broken nose, and a shower of radioactive dust and debris. He is all too aware of time moving, poison accumulating in his blood, bones, like snow. He tells the town, *I stood up and I looked around. . . . I ran through the doorway howling like a wolf.* No one helps him. No one wants to get close. He scrubs himself with dirt and water from a garden hose. He reaches inside his own throat, makes his body vomit, makes the sounds that no one wants to hear. Finally, from the silence, a siren. Lore says the ambulance had to be destroyed after transporting him to Vassar.

He wants us to know. The lake is not a pristine swimming hole that has rinsed itself clean from an unfortunate holiday blunder. The lake holds the material memory of what was made in that incubator. The half-life of plutonium-238 is 87.7 years. *I was frightened for my life,* he says. As are residents. That year, Pawling fourth grader Jennifer Manganello writes a letter to the editor of the *Poughkeepsie Journal* when there are plans to drain Nuclear Lake. She reasons, *All that water will soak into the ground, and go into our wells, and we will burn up. That's what I think.* Because draining the lake means sending that water somewhere. *We'll die if you do drain Nuclear Lake.*

The same week that Parseghian crashes the meeting, my mother gives birth to her final and biggest baby yet. Emily is ten pounds solid and six years my junior. She'll grow up to be a regular-sized nurse, follow in mom's footsteps. In between, I will baby her or mother her. Is there a difference? I will try to teach her how to read, too early. I will make her a beauty pageant sash out of construction paper, a crown of cardboard. I'll tell her to stop being weird, stop thinking that anybody cares about the blush flaring in her cheeks when we walk into the mall. I'll tell her to cheer me up, to leave me alone, to tell me a story, to put on a show, to get over it and stand tall.

The lab at Nuclear Lake no longer stands. All of the buildings are gone, although there are rumors of an underground tunnel that appears on some maps of the site. There are other questions, too, which arise from old aerial photographs studied by Cornell University, photographs originally taken to monitor crops in the area. These snapshots reveal barrels at the site, drums stored outdoors. There, then gone. The photos show pits dug into the ground, then filled, possible burial sites for problem objects? Also, *numerous footpaths leading from facility buildings to the lakeshore.* The photos show that there wasn't a lakeshore, not at first. Nuclear Lake was a sprawling wetland, edges amorphous, until a dam changed the story. And who walks those paths? Do they go to the water for fish? For a swim? For disposal? When the Atomic Energy Commission studies the site, they find *several safety violations* including a failure *to provide a system at the emergency evacuation site to collect drain water from decontamination of personnel.* In other words, whatever poison Parseghian was able to spare his own body went right into those handfuls of dirt he used to scrub himself clean.

And the earth does its thing, in its own time. Not ours. Not in time for the folks who live nearby and wonder about their well water, their summer float in Nuclear Lake, what they inherited, what seeped into Whaley Lake, then Fishkill Creek, then Hudson River, then the mammoth Atlantic. They wonder about their cancer rates, too high, too rare. Or they forget the story, or never heard the story, or don't care to interrogate the myth of a tranquil place in their minds. There's resistance there, a surface tension, like the skin on a body of water. Like a survivor's necessary silence, a scientist's doubt, a Bigfoot's will to remain just out of sight with her family, keeping watch.

When the town of Pawling gives Krasinski permission to film *A Quiet Place* on public land, the Recreation Department agrees to quit trimming the grass, quit taming the lush perimeter of the old barn at Lakeside Park. The vines move right in, get greedy. The green becomes unruly, truly perfect. To make an audience believe in monsters, just show them a home both fully lived-in and forgotten, grown over. See their eyes widen with fear, shine with recognition. They know this one. They've seen it before.

YOU LEARN OTHER THINGS

For Mary Anne Spier in *The Baby-Sitters Club #4: Mary Anne Saves the Day* by Ann M. Martin

The child, Jenny, has a fever. It's 104. You're the babysitter. Maybe the best babysitter. Responsible. Having a dead mother will do that for a girl. Your father doesn't love the idea of you galivanting with the girls in The Baby-Sitters Club at odd hours. Whispering about Stacey's diabetes. Styling Claudia's hair. But he allows it so long as it's making you better at giving care. So long as you keep your skirts modest, wrists free of ornamentation, your braids neat and uncut. You want to handle things and part of handling things means knowing when to ask for help. 104 is too high a fever in the book. You call the ambulance. You save the day. Jenny is going to be fine because you know what fevers can do.

My Nolan was 104 degrees and exactly two years old when he had a seizure. Good seizure. Smart seizure. Protecting the brain from heat. At the dinner table, birthday tater tot in his fist, his gaze surprised, then slack. I raced to unbuckle the booster seat clips as my child turned blue. Frantic phone call, the siren, the standing on the sidewalk waving and waving at the approaching lights.

And so, a few years later, when Silas, flu-ridden, hit 104, and the on-call nurse told me to keep him home, I balked. But Nolan! But *The Baby-Sitters Club #4 Mary Anne Saves the Day!* 104 is bad news! 104 is ambulance! And when he's at 105 and she still said *keep him, count his breaths per minute, you don't want him here where he will probably get sicke*r, I lost trust in the thermometer. I shook it, though it was not the shaking kind. I put it under my own tongue, to test it.

I have broken things with my mouth. Spent popsicle sticks. A Paper Mate pen that filled my cheek with ink. My own teeth, clenched in my sleep. And, as a child, a glass mercury thermometer. It was lovely, the little shatter, the way the silver beaded and raced along the grooves of the braided rug in the living room. I don't remember how much I swallowed, or if my mother had me rinse my poisoned mouth. I don't remember if it was ever determined whether I had a temperature or not. Mostly, I remember the poor rug, blues and greens, rolled up and propped on the deck for several decades. Never replaced. Irreplaceable. Every subsequent scratch on that floor felt like mine. I might as well have dragged my teeth across the hardwood. Such a shame. And had I even been sick? In those days, my mother was keen to keep me home from school. *You look glassy-eyed*, she'd say. *Your lips are pink.* A recently discovered kindergarten report card reveals that I was absent 39 days that year, or more than once per week. How many episodes of *The Price Is Right* did I watch with her? Of *Bonanza*? How many times did she measure my temperature? Was she relieved when it was normal? Was she validated when it was elevated? Maybe this was proof that she had the right instincts as mother, as nurse. That she could read the mysterious weather of her children with only a look.

You were motherless, Mary Anne, and I was jealous. I wanted a quiet home where jewelry was not permitted. I wanted a sad but kind dad to whom I could prove in a book's final chapter, *I'm not a kid anymore!* I didn't want my own mother to die, I just wanted a different mother who had died. I wanted some ghost to point to, a reason for why I was *always so sensitive.* As for my own mother, I wanted her in the chorus of a Broadway musical or calculating insulin doses by hand in a clean, bustling hospital. I wanted her happy more than I wanted her. And I know how horrible that is, now that I'm a mother, too. Because part of me wants them to want me more than they want me to be whole or happy, human or alive.

I was not much of a babysitter. I cared about the wrong things. I let the kids stare at cartoons for hours and was too nervous to help myself to anything in the fridge, no matter how many times they insisted, *Help yourself! Help yourself!* as they hurried out the door. When the father drove me home, without a hint of impropriety, I would glare at him as if he were a pervert. I never had a rate, never charged anything. I just took whatever they handed me, shoved it in my back pocket. I didn't like their kids. Their kids didn't like me. If they went to bed on time, it was out of boredom.

By the end of *Mary Anne Saves the Day*, you loosen your hair. But it takes 56 more books for you to cut it short and play with makeup, and for most of those you are falling in love with Logan and making dinner for your sighing father. In *#52 Mary Anne and 2 Many Babies* (not to be confused with *#34 Mary Anne and Too Many Boys*), you and Logan are paired up for a school assignment. You get fake married and are given a fake baby, a white egg, to care for. You are supposed to be learning the drawbacks of sex, but you don't need to learn that, do you? Perpetually, you are the good girl. Too young and too wise all the same. So you learn other things from the egg. Other people's kids are loud, hearty. Yours will be delicate. Yours will need to be tucked into your purse. Yours will be easy to forget, to fail, to replace. You learn that the most fun you will have in your entire wholesome life will be drinking too much red wine at one of those Paint 'n Sip nights, skinny brush in one hand, egg in the other. You'll sit with Beth from *Little Women* and Violet from *The Boxcar Children*. The maternal, mortal girls. The ones who make beautiful, unnecessary things and save them forever.

LUCK NOW

When she reached the top of the hill, she saw a wood in the distance.
She thought that it looked a safe quiet spot.
~Jemima Puddle-Duck by Beatrix Potter

f I take any heed from Beatrix, I will bring you to life only after boiling your bones and sleeping with them, half-articulated, under my pillow. That was her idea of childhood. Mine might have looked similar had I not felt so brittle next to death. And water. And heat. And sleep. Mine was a pink room stuffed with two sisters. Mine held hampers full of dirty costumes that lay untouched for several years. The clothes we wore we heaped on top between washings. At times of boredom, I would push those to the floor and root. Find the crushed tulle that once held the shape of a skirt. Find the new flesh-pink Capezio tights that I'd torn in the first few minutes of wear, then buried in the hamper to age them, to give them a story of ruin that made sense.

You, dumb duck, were on my shelf. Porcelain, made from bone ash, a trinket. I didn't know your story then, but I recall your beak and bonnet. Your improbable shawl. You were not to be played with, and honestly we didn't want to. My grandmother had been gifting us these figurines for years. It was my mother who loved them, who loved their containers. Glossy little boxes, flawless tissue paper, refolded, stowed away for use in some vague future.

Sixteen. I got the part. You. I was new to modern dance. The bare feet and low squats were a relief to me after the years of tiptoe ballet, which my body, swelling into its new shape, was tired of faking. I had no helium. No longer a skinny-limbed, pot-bellied girl, I became a woman full of eggs, promise of bone.

I danced with the fox, and my delectability went beyond the sage, thyme, mint, parsley, and pair of onions. I felt safe. And I was safe. And that was something. After rehearsal one day he gave me a bag of sugar snap peas from his garden. I had never tried them before and I ate every single one as I drove myself home.

Still I thought the point was to be fattened up and swallowed whole. It was different for you, Jemima. You had no interest in disappearing into any story.

The one you longed to out-tell is the one that says ducks are bad mothers. Bad sitters. Laying eggs willy-nilly, allowing them to go cold, to be stolen by a fox or a farmer's wife. *So it was for your own good*, she would say, carrying you by your hindquarters away from another nest. She'd line up your eggs in a long-handled basket and bring it back to the farmhouse. There, she would candle them. Hold them just close enough to the flame to see inside. The fertile ones seemed to hold a spider or a vein-webbed eye. These she would give the hen to incubate and raise. The rest she would crack into omelets, feed to the farmer.

So you flew off to have your own babies. To see if you could. Isn't that the reason most of us become mothers? And the fox gave you the hiding place. The obvious but luxurious bed of feathers. The fox planned a feast, handed you the list of ingredients to gather. And you gathered them. Beatrix said you were a simpleton. But doesn't it make sense that you would trust the animal that treats you as tenderly as an egg?

Lucky duck, they said. You were spared the violence that befell so many ducks before you. This is luck now. Not being torn apart. Not being taken. Not digging your own fragrant grave, mistaking it for love. Luck.

But the eggs. Well. Dogs will be dogs. You should be grateful that the foxhounds chased away the fox. You should know those eggs were too perfect to protect. And, let's face it, they were unattended. In a sense, they were right about you. You weren't hungry enough. You were already floating away.

One afternoon, in the woods, I found a skull and a hoof, and I carried them home. Thumb through an eye socket. Inner wrist awake to the scraps of tawny fur left on the femur. To me these pieces were neither specimens nor treasures. I held them at a normal distance from my body. It wasn't until my mother said, *Rabies!* that they meant anything to me. *Who knows what licked it,* she said. *It can take a year to get sick*, she said. So for twelve months, I didn't sleep, didn't know how to hold anything alive or recently alive. I carried books into bed, laid them on my belly, crushed my lungs with them, slid them under my pillow. They were simple, predictable shapes to finger in the dark. They didn't have the knobs or handles or sockets that Beatrix held all night.

Another night, many years and lucky bodies later, I wake up to the sound of something metallic. A cooking pot shifting in the dish drainer downstairs? A neighbor's pup at the chain link or a thief at the storm door? A coin dropped, somehow, into the drum of our washing machine? I don't wake my husband. I consider the possibilities as I move to share his pillow, and I just drift off.

In the morning there is snow just like they said there would be snow. It was bound, like a book, to happen. But my boys are taking all the credit. They followed the nonsense rules they learned from their friends. Last night they flushed ice cubes down the toilet. They wore their pajamas inside-out. They slept with spoons under their pillows. Alone upstairs, half-making their beds, I find the one that fell. That sang through our house, moved me towards the warm body beside me.

I carry the spoon downstairs to the kitchen, deem it clean. Put it in my mouth.

WOLFLESS

Many are the deceivers.

~*Red Riding Hood* by Anne Sexton

Y ou think to trick your daughter. To teach her a lesson. To lessen her. She's too good, this girl, too trusting. She needs to learn, as girls learn, that a bright hooded cape won't keep her safe in the woods. More often than not, it'll be draped over a rock, studded with briars, or torn, a strip of rich red dangling from the barbed wire fence she scales to reach the better flowers—the *bloodroot, bunchberry, dogtooth*.

Disguises come easy. Red sees you as wolf, not mother, and all it takes is skipping lipstick and bra, parting your hair along a new path, letting your shins grow the fur they want to grow. You don't even alter your voice when you greet her. *Good day*. She takes no pause, greets you back, even shows you where she is headed. *There, among the roots and trunks.*

•

The womb is not a clock, says Anne Sexton. But it will keep time. With both of my babies, my labor came precisely on my due date. I was ready for the pain, but not the grief of being flipped inside out. And not the afterbirth, the way my midwife worried her cold fingers into my belly as if it were a mound of uncooperative dough, until I delivered my placenta into a bedpan. She fished it out, held it up for me to see. I looked past my new baby to study my guts, brandished like a gown. They were the beauty. They were the blame. I had been told I would see the tree of life here. And indeed, the umbilical cord formed a trunk, real roots. The capillaries reached like branches reach. But it was no tree to me. It was, *Oh*, a forest, a place to go missing. A bright red hot wet cape.

My friends took their placentas home with their babies. They buried them under new ginkgo trees or had them desiccated and encapsulated into pills. They swallowed themselves every morning for a month, washed themselves down with gulps of special tea—raspberry leaf, blessed thistle. But I let mine tumble into a 30-gallon garbage bag, as I would any massive, damning evidence. I cut the cord myself. I let my midwife come at me with scissors, thread. A third-degree tear, needle through muscle. I called my mother.

•

In documentary footage, Sexton and her daughter stall at their own front door. Sexton says, *Tell them we're fake!* She eggs her on. *We're fake!* Until the girl agrees, *Fake!* They show obvious affection, take pleasure in shouting, *We hate each other! Despise each other! We just can't bear each other!* They nuzzle together, laugh. The girl disappears inside the house. Sexton goes on. Her voice is rich, theatrical, straight from a 1940s switchboard girl connecting your call. *It's so easy to be natural, when you've got this.* She means her daughter. *I mean, that's for real!* Inside, at her desk, she tries to read a poem aloud, but is interrupted by a barking dog. *Should I let the damn dog in?* she says, annoyed. A look in her eye, into the camera. *I'm peering at the dog, not you.* A beat. *Right?* Back in her poem, a mother poem, she calls, *My carrot, my cabbage!* She asks, *Will I give you my eyes?*

•

You get the idea packing Red up for a visit to Gram, who is sick again, like her mother before, always ailing. A cruel stitch in her belly or a godawful headache or a heart gripped with anxiety you can't bear to sit beside. You are grateful that the girl is old enough to send on her own. If your daughter does nothing more than save you from a conversation with Gram, you will deem motherhood worth the trouble. But is she quite ready? You've been wrong before. The time when she was just a toddler and she took off on her trike. That hill, that scrape on her face. And the stories that bored her, the poems with the words she had no interest in sounding out. She was teaching you. Not everybody wants to know everything.

•

When I was a teenager, a little girl went missing. It was all over the news. Her mother's grief was all over the news, a cloak. When they dug up the little body, stuffed in a garbage bag, they found that the girl's mouth had been duct-taped shut. Everyone blamed the mother, who admitted to the burial but not the murder, insisting that the girl was already dead. She had no explanation for the duct tape. My sisters and I relished our outrage, but our mother told us to hold our judgment. What did we know? Maybe the mother couldn't bear the thought of her daughter's mouth filling with bugs. Even if that mouth was dead. Even if those bugs would get in there eventually. She told us it was a horrible thing for a mother to imagine. Which of course made us imagine it, too. That girl's mouth. Kept quiet. Twitching with life.

•

Red doesn't ask, *Where's the aspirin? The penicillin? Where's the fruit juice?* Still, she clocks the wine and cake for what they are. Bookends to a feast, treats, nothing that can make a person better. Nothing like the pink stuff or the horse pills or the heady ointments that have dressed Red's wounds.

You meant to keep the lesson small. In the forest, you would steal the basket. Leave her cakeless, wineless. Maybe even lost. She would turn wise, guarded. This would make her safe. And you would reveal yourself, you would, once you'd polished off the cake you made, reddened the forest floor with the wine you never liked. She would see you as mother. She would be grateful when you returned the empty basket, grateful to have a way to carry the wilting flowers to Gram, who would feel her own disappointment, no doubt, but who doesn't have some little hurt waiting up ahead through the trees?

What you failed to imagine: That Red would never put the basket down. That when you found her in the woods, she would have already left the path of her own accord, that the girl would lure herself. And why wouldn't she stop for a spontaneous bouquet? You are not the only one hunting for a remedy.

·

Sexton loves her poems, doesn't want to throw any of them away. She says, *I didn't know what was good and bad for a long time. I still don't.* In the footage, she grows distracted by a classical piano recording. This tune is *like sex! I mean it's like the most beautiful! Like my daughter! Anything living! This* song is *better than a poem! Music beats us!*

After Sexton's death, the tapes from her therapy sessions go public. In some, she's been hypnotized, given sodium pentothal—truth serum. In some, she details her abuse as a child. In some, she admits to abusing her daughter. Sexton kills herself. Her daughter writes the story. Inherits the story, inhabits the story. Car humming in the garage, blood running in the bathtub. Mother, daughter. No one *unhaunted.* When they find the dead poet, she is dressed in her mother's fur coat.

·

You beat Red to the cottage, which is new but built to look old. Gram has the notion that *nothing haunts a new house.* She is wrong.

You're in the door before she can shuffle into her slippers. *So it's you, old sinner*, she says. Are you wolf to her? Are you daughter? There is only time to be both at once. The windows are open, always open, and you hear Red singing as she comes up the path.

You tell Gram to hide. She obliges. It must be her turn to disappear. She steps out of her slippers, out of her nightdress. She helps you pull it over your head. She hands you the matching sleep cap and climbs into your mouth, unhappy. If you wanted her dead, you would bite down now, but you swallow instead. *It's as fast as a slap.*

A new belly. *What big*, you say. *The better to!* as you labor across the floorboards, towards the tiny brass bed, once yours. It is plenty big enough for Gram, who prides herself on how little she longs for. She never dreams, never flips onto her belly, never flips her pillow to feel cloth gone cold. She's not like you, full of need. *The bed is stale with your childhood.* You settle in just as Red lifts the latch.

•

Red has never been my color. Redheads, as a rule, can't pull it off. We're too pale. Too strange. Too blue of vein. Red is nothing but clash. But the hair, called red but not red, I grew it past my waist. My mother said it was too beautiful to cut, and I believed her. When, after more than a decade, it grew heavy, I protested. This was too much for a girl to carry. This was Rapunzel territory. My mother relented, cut it herself to the middle of my back. Light hit the scissors. She wrapped the bright braid in foil, tucked it into a drawer where it would darken, dullen. Was it still mine, this pelt in a chest?

Later, love. One who saw nothing special in my hair, whose eyes could not distinguish among red, green, brown. If I was red, then the grass was red. If I was red, then so were the woods.

But I get ahead of my story.

•

What big teeth you have, you say to Red, who uses them to tear the foil from the wine. Who knows her way around a corkscrew. She smiles your wide smile, her milk teeth long gone. She pours an inch of wine into a teacup, the way Gram likes it, carries it to the bed with a bite of cake on a plate. She gives it to you, compliments your grandest features, then turns to search through your cabinets for a canning jar. This wild bouquet needs a home.

•

If you gave my mother flowers, she would see them as a burden. Now she had to dig out a vase, find a blade to trim the stems. Now she had to fill another vessel. Now she had to put a pretty thing on a table, watch it wither.

They say a daughter steals your beauty. If you're pregnant, and ugly, there's a girl in there. It's a lie. My mother stayed lovely, even as we donned her small shoulders and feet, her big brains and strong legs. Her arthritis. Rosacea. Her hot, sad stare out a picture window. I once showed her a photograph I took of her on the beach. She failed to recognize herself. She could have been anyone. And I, in the mirror, see my own body's surrender. How the flesh grows disinterested in the bones, wanders off. How the skin around my eyes, inherited, welcomes its doom to pillow and droop. Hell, I was only sixteen when an optometrist suggested I might like an eye lift. *What big eyes!* Maybe I wanted a little tuck, a pinch at the corners of my lids to make me better?

•

Red should get home. The light outside is fading. She has regaled you with stories about school and braids and boys and wolves, more than she ever shared with you as her mother. Skip the trick, you decide, and you ask her to stay. Tell her to hang up her cloak for goodness sake, to polish off the cake because Lordy knows you don't need it. You don't need anything.

She hangs her cloak but declines the cake. Her mother, she confesses, bakes everything wrong. She goes to her basket, pulls out handfuls of earth. Here is what she really loves. *Mushrooms,* she says. She found them *pulsing inside the moss.*

•

The girl lodges in your throat. From within you, some growl. You think of the early days, when she'd pretend a doorway was her picture frame, when she'd climb halfway up, bracing herself. A leg on each side. Or her back against one side, feet together on the other. You'd find her, posed, waiting to be found. Pretending to read a book mid-levitation. Demanding a secret password to let you pass. And once you tickled her armpit, in a mean but deniable way, and she fell like you knew she would fall.

She drops past your heart, settles in with Gram. What else is lost inside of you? *Where is the moral?* Whatever you say, they will hear it. You remember that much from pregnancy. Little ears are big ears. No whisper goes unheard. And while *many are the deceivers,* even liars say what's true.

•

Once, my mother played a prostitute in a community theater production of the old musical *Bells Are Ringing.* The plot centers on Ella, a young woman working for a telephone answering service. Ella tries on several voices, a different self for every client. She falls in love with a caller while masquerading as an old woman. She follows that love, has to reckon with her lie. Along the way, a detective has a hunch that this answering service is actually a front for an escort service. And so there was my mother, stage left, suggestively twirling a long beaded necklace. Part of a crowd, a pack of other middle-aged mothers from my town, hands on hips, lips pursed. Pretending to be prostitutes. Or women mistaken for prostitutes. *Suburban matrons,* who, for one night, had simply chosen *cocktail parties* over *cottage* and *supermarket.* There was nothing cartoonish about my mother up there. She was a beauty. It was the only time in my life I saw her put her body on display, and I remember wondering if she did this sort of thing in the mirror when we were at school. If she caught her own eye, *letting her stomach fill up with helium.* Letting her limbs go *loose as kite tails.*

Once, she died a little on a hospital table and she floated above her body. It was not unpleasant. Once, her dead grandmother appeared at the foot of her childhood bed on Florence Road. It was a comfort. Once, she pulled a story out of my hands. She wanted me to know that her mother read books. That's all she did. Read books and cried. It was a warning.

●

Not all knives are for stabbing, but this one is. The huntswoman licks the blade, caked in cake, and her tongue is spared. She's been drawn by your snore, too much wolf for her liking. She sees Red's cloak, hears the chatter in your belly. *It's as simple as opening a letter.*

Babies cry when born, but Red and Gram are laughing, some new tether between them, as they step out of the basket of your ribcage, push aside the curtains of your belly flesh. This wide open is worse than the blade, and you cannot bear to look as the others set to work on your body. Somebody shaves your legs, colors your lips. Somebody embraces you; it must be Red. Somebody fills you up with rocks. You will never be empty again. You remember this is how they did away with witches once. *Rock climbs on rock,* a lesson in fits and starts. Then there is the stitching. Gram's deft hand, no doubt. She once showed you how to mend, but you refused to learn. She gathers your flesh, your skin, her own nightgown with the needle. Your eyes go last.

Then, a party? The clinking of glasses. The pouring of more wine, some red reserve you didn't know Gram kept. More cake, mushrooms, wedges of cheese pulled out of the icebox. Crusty bread sliced, then torn. Meat, from some animal, sizzles in a pan. No one discusses you. You are already a memory, a premonition. A figure in a story. And so the harm you have caused is unforgivable. But also forgettable, for those who tend to forgetting. It's not the lesson you dreamed up, but it's what the girl learns.

•

Sexton is haunted. But she tells the camera, *I'm not going to spend my life researching to see if I can get related to a Salem witch. Probably.* It's not entirely clear if she means she probably won't spend her life doing so or if she reasons that, in all likelihood, she is related to a Salem witch.

Like me. My ancestor was a grandmother when she was accused, tried, and killed in Salem. We have so many mothers.

•

They leave you in the cottage, under some old blanket. It smells of butter, sinew, spirits, the residue of all they wolfed down. Then it hits you. This is the cloak. Red won't wear it again, this gift you gave her. Which Gram gave you. Which Great Gram tied around her own tender throat with a satin ribbon, long since lost to the whims of the woods. This might be love. This might be *womb, clock, bell.* Wearing it, you are willing to be the villain. To have eyes so big, a mouth so big, you can fit the truth inside.

Yes, it was red.

•

Once, or over and over, a mother went to her sewing stash, pulled out her brightest bolt of fabric. She cut it to fit you, to find you. She marked you as a target. If there were wolves they stayed wolves, and away. They knew about mothers. Mothers will swallow you whole.

WHAT THE
DEAD KNOW
BY ACT THREE

Just open your eyes, dear. That's all.

~Myrtle Webb in *Our Town* by Thornton Wilder

Mama, am I pretty?
I'm Emily Webb, stringing invisible green beans in Grover's Corners at the turn of the century. My voice? Trying to achieve the Down East New England accent learned from a cassette played in my pink Casio tape deck. I'm not great. *Mama* makes me sound not South Maine but South South. *Designing Women* South. My beans are worse than my accent. In my seventeen years I've never handled fresh green beans and so my pantomime looks more sorcery than kitchen chore. It's not that my family doesn't cook vegetables. We just prefer cut and frozen, stopped in time until the moment we are hungry, ready. Birds Eye.

What the dead know by Act Three is that the living lack perspective. They miss the gift of each moment as it happens. When

I tell you, my mother Myrtle Webb, that I have lost my blue hair ribbon, you know where it is. *Just open your eyes, dear, that's all. I laid it out for you, special. On the dresser, there. If it were a snake, it would bite you.* What is mundane for alive Emily overwhelms dead Emily. I can't bear the love, the lack. I lift the imaginary ribbon, tie it to the end of my braid.

My mind carries a map of my children's objects. The ten-dollar bill that slipped out of Nolan's birthday card is on the third shelf of the hutch under a blue pencil sharpener. The green balloon is on top of the refrigerator with the old Halloween candy after too much fighting. Two pairs of sneakers sat out in the rain last night beside the sandbox. One shoe has been carried a few feet away from the others. Maybe some night animal.

My own mother lacked this map, or lost it through mothering seven children and their wreckage. If anything, she came to us for lost objects. Pens, certain serving spoons, potentially lucky mailings from Publishers Clearing House.

We weren't big on hair ribbons, but ballet recital season gave us Sucrets tins full of bobby pins. My hair fell to my waist, heavy. Buns gave me terrible headaches, but they were worth the version of myself that my mother called beautiful. There is something to that. A mother's hands in your hair and then her mouth saying those words.

One morning, no performance in sight, my mother dries my hair in the dining room. I am in second grade. Jealous of my older siblings who seem to have more purpose in life than me, I have started inventing elaborate homework assignments for myself. First, a book report on *Ribsy* where I simply retype several chapters. This morning, a telling-time assignment where I am required, I say, to draw an analog clock for every single hour and minute combination. I trace an upside-down jar of Skippy for the circle, use a short ruler to make the hands perfect. I have dozens of looseleaf pages going, pencil shavings sprinkled here and there when the tip gets dull. I tell my mother that these clocks are due today and I am just too busy for the hair dryer. Although she is a nurse, my mother has her own theory of infectious disease which seems mostly tied to wet hair in winter. So she dries my hair for me. She is tender and she is not tender. She is beginning to question this homework assignment, calls it ridiculous, but seems to admire my uncharacteristic diligence. She moves the hair dryer in figure eights, a magic wand. She doesn't want to burn me. I sit at the dining room table and make clock after clock in the hot wind. The memory ends here. There's no way I finish. Maybe I confess that I made these clocks for myself. That I made them so I could throw them away.

You, Myrtle, are played by a kind but forgettable woman. I can't conjure her face. But she sits beside me, wearing an apron, when I ask about my beauty. You are good with the green beans. You snap the end, zip the string off, toss what's ready in the basket. Your goal, you've told Mrs. Gibbs, is to *put up forty quarts if it kills me*. But I'm the one who dies first. Childbirth. If the baby makes it, the play doesn't say, but I leave a four-year-old son in the world of the living. When, from the grave, I get to choose a memory to return to, I pick my own childhood, not his. I pick my twelfth birthday. I declare everybody beautiful.

In college, when I'm still doing plays but not yet writing poetry, I get my first real haircut. My mother has trimmed my hair about once a year since I was eleven, but I have never had the salon treatment. I don't want anything fussy. I was raised to care about clothes and makeup only when getting on a stage. I tell the hairdresser to cut it to my shoulders. No layers. No face-framing, whatever that is. There is no reason to pay thirty dollars for a straight chop, but I do. It's a mistake. When I see my mother over break, she tells me, *You look utterly nondescript*. I savor my hurt and I know she is wrong. I have huge eyes and bad acne. I have a conspicuously plain haircut and my hair is bright orange. My forehead is high, my gums show when I smile, and all of my pants are too long. I am descript as hell.

I don't have any daughters to disappoint. All of my lovelys and beautifuls are given to my boys, not that they want them. *Stop*, they whine, *We're not.* I suppose all of us are doomed to get it wrong, to keep filling the basket with the wrong invisible props. As George Gibbs tells me over strawberry phosphates at the soda shop, *I guess new people aren't any better than old ones.*

You have a rule. No books at the table. You say you'd rather have your children healthy than bright. The implication, I suppose, is that your children will forget to eat, to stay alive, if they are caught up in some story. But even the breakfast itself is a fabrication, nothing more than a tale we tell ourselves in the morning. I wear a wedding dress but I'm divorcing from everything I've been clinging to. I say goodbye to breakfast, to food and coffee. To clocks ticking and to the sunflowers you grow in our garden. I say goodbye to sleeping and I say goodbye to waking up.

But not before you answer my question.

Mama, am I pretty?

When you do, you are as honest as the living can be.

You're pretty enough for all normal purposes.

TWENTY
WENDYS

Stars are beautiful, but they may not take an active part in any-thing, they must just look on forever.

~J. M. Barrie, *Peter Pan*

One

The Lost Boys don't know a single story. That's why Peter's been coming around the Darling window, scattering sheer skeleton leaves on the sill. Mother holds story time every night and Pan wants in. But when he cries, it's not about mothers, he insists. He cries because the soap won't marry his shadow to the soles of his feet. And besides, he isn't crying. Shadows are overrated. Shadows don't make you real. They only reveal how little you're lit from within. Mothers are overrated, too, although he concedes that, as a rule, *one girl is of more use than twenty boys*. Which twenty? Wendy wants to know. Her sleeping brothers, plus eighteen more? Or the boys who have been tugging at her manicotti curls on the school bus? The ones who ask her if the curtains match the carpet before she has any idea what they are talking about? Or maybe twenty men? Kind ones? Drunk ones? Twenty Lost Boys?

There are no Lost Girls. Peter says girls are too clever to fall out of their prams, abandon their parents when they hear discussion of their future. Girls don't book it when they learn it's just a matter of time until they're sewing a boy's shadow in place, pushing a pram of their own. Girls stay. Girls tend, fix. Even Tinkerbell gets her name from tinkering, mending the pots and kettles back in Neverland. But that's not a story, not one a mother would tell. That's just life.

Two

Before she became a mother, Mary Darling found herself drawing pictures of babies without faces. Were they too difficult to imagine? Or did she worry she would jinx their perfection by sketching it on the back of her list of errands? Nevertheless, she got Wendy, John, and Michael. All robust enough to be left in the care of a St. Bernard. All sufficiently nimble that they learn to fly in a single, complimentary lesson.

Wendy imagines more. A house of leaves sewn together. An orphan wolf for a pet. She makes what she will of a thimble. It's a kiss. It's a hook. She'll trade it for whatever the world offers, to a point. When the mermaids taunt her, douse her with the Neversea, she makes a weapon out of a conch, waves it above her head in a fury. Says *If. You. Ever.* Wendy's a drag in that prim nightgown. The mermaids sulk. They were only trying to drown her.

Three

The lesbians invite my sister and me to the movies and my parents allow us to go. Nina and Gina are our next-door sinners, but I suppose you can hate the sin and love that the sinner will get your kids out of the house for a few hours in the summertime. One of them is handy and one wears dresses and I always get it wrong. Their niece and nephew are visiting. Elevenish, like us. Before heading to the movie theater, we kids take turns stretching out on huge sheets of paper on the floor and tracing one another's bodies. I fill in the blank shape I've made. A face that's older than mine. A necklace I don't own. A twirly skirt, also made-up.

Three towns over, on the big screen, *Hook*. Julia Roberts is Tinkerbell. Dustin Hoffman is Captain Hook. Robin Williams is Peter—a grown-up, a father who has forgotten himself. Who has to save his own lost children. *Boy, why are you crying*, asks Maggie Smith, an ancient Wendy, tasked with waking Peter up to his past. He's angry with her for being the wrong kind of girl. The kind that sweeps up fairy dust after an adventure. The kind that grows old. I can't help but hate her a little bit, too. No ribbons, just wrinkles. A place I never want to go.

I swoon over a Lost Boy in a checkered blazer. I study Nina and Gina in the dark. There is an ease between them, a togetherness that hooks my heart. Will they belong to each other when they are old? When half the world doesn't want them? I've seen the TV specials. Sandy Duncan, Mary Martin, Cathy Rigby. Their Peters, their strings showing when they fly. Boy or girl. Young or old. Wendy or Tink. Peter or Pan. We see what the story demands: fairies when we clap for fairies. Shadows when shadows elude us.

Four

The first boy I love is a boy in tights. An accomplished dancer whom everyone reads as gay but me. Matthew is built like a gymnast—broad shoulders, tapered trunk—and wears soft sweaters that smell of CK One. All it takes is the heat of his hand on my forearm and I am in it. We're theater kids, of course we are. And before he kisses me behind the high school, he says he is nervous. Says he is chicken shit. And I might even say it back. That I'm chicken shit. That the two of us, under these blurry stars, are chicken shit. And I let him kiss me, even though this is my first-ever kiss and it will always be shadowed by these words. Chicken. Shit.

Our official romance is brief but we are in some kind of love for a few years. Matthew visits me at the toy store where I work after school. At night, I let the phone cord curl around each of my fingers and think of his fingers and listen to his voice—fast, low. He wears a tie to dinner one night as a joke. Or it's not a joke and I hurt him assuming it is. He takes another girl to his winter formal. He drives to my house late one summer night to swim. And another night in tears. He's caught wind of a rumor about him and another boy and *it's a horrible lie, Marianne.* He was always saying my name. *It's not true, Marianne. I know,* I say. I don't say what I know. I don't know what I know.

We go on like this until he goes to college, goes on to dance in New York. He gives me his number and I write it down to rip it up and I tell him so. That he had better call me first, since I'm the girl left behind. I'm mean. I love him. And I suspect he is about to leave me forever.

We meet once or twice after. We've forgotten how long to hold each other and what it means. Even so, this boy is a goddamn rooster. He wakes me up to my body. He leaves for the last time for the twinkling city where he dreams up new ways for bodies to move. And then moves them.

Five

I lie to the doctor. Tell him that I fell. Or that I was attempting some acceptable childhood trick, a flip, a handstand. The truth? I tried to fly. Climbed up on the hearth without a thought and launched myself, face-first, into the hardwood floor as if it were an ocean. I am far too old—five or six—to see Peter and Wendy as possibility. Too old to believe that I can think happy thoughts, that I arrived in this world with a fixed shimmer of pixie dust on my inner wrists, behind my ears.

It's the hinge of my jaw that is of concern. It clicks when I open my mouth, but not when I close it. It's a tick without a tock and there's no figuring it out. The doctor sends me home with my mother, who enjoys this other side of injury, and regales me all the way home with the stories of hospital visits. Births—waters breaking, babies rushing. Hurts—David after the sled, Amy after the staircase. After, I clench my teeth for thirty years and counting. Maybe I'm a crocodile. You smash your face and this is your new face.

Six

Yet I flew all of the time as a child. Ask Amy. So many nights, we had the same dreams, hands clasped, floating past the ceiling fan. Most of my dreams were set in my home and I never touched down. If I wasn't flying above the clutter, I was swimming, my house a sea. A therapist would have a field day with that one, friends say. And friends who are therapists agree. Field day. Therapists stand in the heat, waiting for their turn on the obstacle course. They cradle eggs in spoons, tie their ankles together with twine. Potato sacks materialize, as do water balloons. Therapists hide under the parachute. Their hands blister on the rope they pull together. They have never been so strong. They are a team, a family. They feel that tug of love. That tug of war. They enjoy wedges of watermelon at the end, although the flesh is warm, and full of seeds, and there are bees nearby.

Seven

My father has never forgiven 7 Up. Once upon a time, he had pitched them an ad campaign based on our family, the Uphams. We were seven kids and at least three of us could carry a tune. In his mind, we were the do-re-mi Von Trapps, minus the Nazis and short a few costumes cut from drapery. We could be, can't you imagine it, *The Singing 7 Ups*. We'd have a jingle. Then maybe a chart-topping single. We'd have a lifetime supply of a beverage we didn't care for but the sheer excess, the glowing bottles stacked in the portico, would feel like wealth. But the company turned us away and the dream receded. It went to the place where Dad almost made it to *Jeopardy!* To where a talent scout gave my mother a business card after Emily shined as Wendy on stage. To the time my ballet teacher who took the train from the city asked me to come train in the city and neither my mother nor I believed enough in my talent. The Uphams would never be stars.

In school, on afternoons when teachers grow tired and hoarse, kids play the 7-Up game. They rest on their desks, heads in arms. They mash their eyes into the crooks of their elbows until they see constellations. They try to sleep or they stick up a thumb, wishing. Pick me, pick me.

Eight

We have a Peter. My parents' golden child. Left us at fourteen for boarding school. Would show up on holidays, breeze through in summertime. Once, he arrived after a climbing adventure. Tucked in his duffel bag, a brown bat. He was proud to have a stowaway; it was proof that he was of another world. Not a world where boys stayed boys, but one where they grew up early. Left the house in the woods where the shades were drawn and the attic was ceded to the mice and wasps. Left the bickering and television, the ticks and the phobias. Left the six of us singing the theme song to *Eight Is Enough* because if we counted our parents as children, it worked.

The bat, we killed it. It took a battle with a broom under the naked kitchen lightbulb. My father, his shadow. The bat, her shadow. Things ended in the dining room. My father invited us to look at the small body on the floor. He was not proud, but relief can look like pride. My mother warned us not to touch it, not to enter the room for months, not to catch the diseases that flying things carry. Why didn't we catch the bat and set it free? Why didn't we open a window?

There is a photo I used to sit with. It shows Peter, thirteen, asleep on Dad's recliner in the afternoon. He holds me, an infant, a weight on his chest. My limbs are folded, my skin so pale, so thin, you might see through to my bones. I am awake, keeping him.

Nine

How many of us have been the reluctant mother to a pack of boys? There's Wendy. She's crawled down into the hollowed-out tree where they sleep. Tootles, Nibs, Slightly, Curly, The Twins, John, Michael, and Peter of course. Wendy readies them for bed. It's been but one day and little Michael has already forgotten his real mother back home, pins it all on Wendy. *Mother*, he says. *Remember*, she says. The other boys don't know the word. *Mother? What's Mother?* Wendy admonishes them through song: *What makes mothers all that they are? Might as well ask what makes a star.* It's an impossible question.

Nevertheless, they seem to get it. With mothers, you wash off the war paint. Your arrow feels stupid in your hand and you snap it in half, leave the mess on the floor for her to tidy. With mothers, you fall asleep in a fox costume even though you intend to play and fight forever. You don't stand a chance against a mother's soprano in the dark of a gutted sycamore.

It's called Hangman's Tree, and there's a rope at the ready. For whom. Hook and his crew find the hideout. They stand outside, cock their heads to hear Wendy's song floating up. All of the pirates grow wistful, suspended by the melody, but Smee goes overboard. He bawls, has to lift his striped t-shirt to catch his tears. There's his big soft belly. And there's the tattooed heart, the banner curled in the wind, baring the word. Mother.

Ten

I'm snatched up from a nap by a scream from my toddler's bedroom. Terror. I book it up the stairs, throw open the door and don't know what I see. Something is in Nolan's crib and it isn't Nolan. It's a ghost, a shrieking cocoon. It is some creature being born, or newly swallowed, and where is my boy? Gone in some other mother's stroller? Out the window? And what on earth has she left in his place?

Until it's Nolan, who, somehow, has burrowed under the white fitted crib sheet without disturbing the elastic corners. Or possibly has re-tucked them from underneath? Either way, he can't find his way out.

And I admit that I enjoy our distress for a beat. It is so easy to fix, this plummet in my gut, it's already happening. His cries, his fear trapped in the white, in the bars of the crib, out it will all go, quick as a wished-upon birthday candle. Such pleasure in my tiny capability. What's a sheet pulled aside, two hands, stars, a breast, a verse of *How I Wonder?* I laugh as I make it across the room to him. Before I even set him free I am in tears, in stitches.

Eleven

One winter, I learn to sew. My brain is too broken by babies to write a word, but I need to make something or I will go mad. My teacher admits that she took up the thimble, the needle, when she was home with an infant. *Babies are boring,* she said. *And they sleep a lot.* I have heard of such babies. Mythical babies, fairy babies. But mine is sleep-starved. And I have never felt so fragile, like a shadow pulled across a snowy mountain. Any stretch of rest beyond three hours eludes me. I'm never fully awake. My limbs are difficult to organize, false starts when I go to pick up my son, who waves his arms at me like a plane-crash survivor. My hands feel heavy, mittened, useless as hooks.

The rotary cutter is a force I can trust. I buy beautiful fabric and slice it into long, rolling ribbons. I make a few quilts, a birthday banner. I jam the machine and spill a thousand pins where my boy is learning to crawl. I make curtains printed with black birds and orange teardrops. Notice how big prints pair well with tiny ones. Fussy-cut to preserve the image of a Victorian woman falling through blue, but fail to account for seam allowance and her head disappears into the blanket. I notice new muscle memory. Release the safety on the cutter. Wind a bobbin. Reach for a scrap, a leader, a spider. Chain-piece.

Across the room is my son, in some contraption. He would rather be in my arms. *I am keeping you safe*, I might say, a blade in my hand. *I am making you something lovely. I love you.* Blood on my thumb.

Twelve

Wendy goes to say her full name. She loves the rhythm of it. Wendy, Moira, Angela, Darling. It's a heart beating, wings beating, but Peter waves her off. *Wendy's enough.* Years later, her lover, her pirate, her therapist all offer these same words to her. They never land the way the men imagine they will land. Off she storms, not to tell herself stories, not to say this to a mirror after a shower. She does not need to learn that she is adequate. Wendy is not enough. Wendy is too much, already. They only think they've seen her fly.

Thirteen

The girl is almost thirteen. To mark the occasion, her father has promised no more nights in the nursery. Instead, a room where she can be alone, free of brothers and stories. Wendy is no stranger to gifts that aren't. She's learned that a glittery new pencil case means summer is dying and she is bound for penmanship exercises. She's undone the ribbon on a pillowy package of sanitary pads. Just for you, her mother had said. Not to share with your brothers. She knows but she still can't help herself. The new room waits in her imagination. Windowless, but hers. She will figure out where girls buy posters and buy one depicting a boy band she has heard of but never heard. She will forfeit penny candy and save her coins for dream catchers. When she goes for a Neverland visit one spring, she'll bring the prettiest one as a gift for Tiger Lily. The princess will accept it, declaring the dream catcher the whitest gift she has ever received. Wendy hears this as praise. She smiles, blushes. *Oh, Wendy*, says Tiger Lily. *No need to get red in the face.*

When the spring cleaning is complete and it is time for Wendy to fly back to London, she is in a mood. Her expectations haven't quite panned out. Lost Boy toilets have lost their luster. To cheer her, Peter brandishes a clutch of colorful feathers. From Tiger Lily, he says. Wendy perks up, rubs pixie dust into her pulse points. Do they have any special meaning? *Sure,* says Peter. *I mean, some of them. Not all of them.* Wendy wears her favorites home in her hair. When she's closing in, soaring over the Thames, she admires the way they change the shape of her shadow on the water.

Fourteen

The order is clear—Kill the Wendy-Bird. It's no bird, anyone can see. It's a girl in a nightgown, still getting the hang of her body in the sky. But the boys trust Tink's bells over their own sight, and Tootles lifts his bow, his arrow, and shoots her down.

Nothing is unforgivable in Neverland, not a bounty, not a hit. Even when Tink gives up the hideout, hoping Hook will end the girl for good, she's not worried. Peter will forget. Tootles will, too. He'll marry Wendy when the time comes. He'll shoot the game they serve at the wedding feast.

Hook boxes up a time bomb. Ties a ribbon around it, a trick, a gift for Peter. Hook hangs the package from a rope, from his hook, and lowers it into the hideout. A tick for a tock. A clock for a crocodile. Tinkerbell gets wind of it, races to her boy, and saves him although he doesn't deserve saving. Who leaves Neverland to poach a mother from London? Who forgets that his mother is already here glowing, who grows deaf to her voice, hearing only a shake of bells? Okay, fine, so she is smaller than she thought she'd be. She is not as kind or as fun. Her need for applause is incessant. But they belong to each other. Hasn't she lit every ship in his sea?

Fifteen

The quickening begins early in the second trimester. My baby boy is the size of a fairy in there. His movements feels like a tugging, like he is lugging around a rope in fits and starts, tying knots to hunker down. He seems to be sticking around, despite the cramping and bleeding that is pale pink, pretty. When things feel too still, I drink orange juice over ice to make him dance.

Pregnancy can be a great surrender, and I'm ever curious about these two new bodies—mine, my growing baby's. Appetites flare. In a matter of days, hormones render me limber beyond anything I could achieve in fifteen years of ballet. My hair is thick as drapery, my mood as light and fragile as a moth. After a streak of insomnia, my capacity for sleep becomes otherworldly. Nothing can wake me.

I take credit for whatever it is my body is doing. *I gave our kid eyelashes today,* I say to Rob. *Little McGillicutty has fingerprints and a nervous system. You're welcome.* The midwife measures my belly with the same tape measure for sale at the fabric shop. *A little big,* she says. *Ever so slightly. He's going to be a good size.*

Sixteen

Her choice: the pen or the plank. Sign on to Hook's crew or meet Davy Jones at the bottom of the sea. She chooses plank, good form, and her bound hands behind her back are fixed like another lovely bow. She goes with dignity, chin high. No one has to push her off the edge. It's inevitable at this point. There's no difference between a fall and a jump. She steps. Plummets. Hook cups his ear to listen for her splash, but it doesn't come. The crew is flummoxed. No splash? Not a ripple? They're spooked. *It's a jinx,* they say, the ship bewitched.

And it is. Pan's a ghost come back, a shadow in the sail. He cuts it with his dagger, crows.

Seventeen

The Lost Boys slaughter pirates, and Slightly keeps count. Twelve, thirteen, fourteen. The battle is what you would expect. Ragtag boys in the crow's nest, pirates climbing a lattice of rope, knives clenched between their teeth. The boys embrace gravity for once, sending down spitballs and makeshift billy clubs, cannonballs and John's umbrella. Fifteen. Tink gets in on the action. Sixteen. Wendy vanishes like any savvy mother. Let the battle toughen them and soften them. She's done her part. She's walked the plank and set an example. Let them learn from each other now. Let her skirt the blame.

But then Peter gets braggy, promises Hook, *one hand tied behind my back!* And Wendy can't stay gone. She materializes in the crow's nest—we never see how—and she warns him, *No, Peter! It's a trick!*

She wants to be on the other side of saved. On the other side of Neverland. Baby Michael, who sleeps with a stuffed bear, has just killed a pirate with a cutlass he lifted from a corpse. This simply won't do. It is time to get to the final body count, to calculate how many things they will need to forget in order to remember home.

Peter stays true to his word. One hand. No pixie dust. And in no time at all, Pan's pinned Hook to the ground, tied him up in the Jolly Roger flag, a skull-and-bones present for the hungry sea, which swallows him whole.

Seventeen! announces Slightly.

Only two pirates survive—Starkey and Smee. Both flee in the tender: Starkey, to be captured by the island tribe, Smee to the shore to trade pirate stories for shillings. He likes the song they make together. When he empties his pockets into a metal bowl on his night stand, the coins ring like bells, clang like tiny weapons.

The Lost Boys cheer. The ship is theirs. They steer her. They feel like men.

Eighteen

Silas is two when he moves into his big-kid bed. One night, he is inconsolable. Is he hurt? No. Does he miss the crib? No. His anguish comes from his inability to climb his bedroom wall, to reach the ceiling. He can find nothing to grasp. A running start does nothing. He seems to think he has done it before, if only he could remember how.

Does he fly in his dreams? Does he forget which life is his real life?

By five, he is in love with battle. Every stick he can lift is a sword. He fishes a heavy knife out of the kitchen drawer, to feel what it feels like in the palm of his hand.

Who will you fight, Silas?

Bad guys, Mama.

Or maybe it's *Bad guys. Mama.* The start of a list.

Nineteen

The crocodile doesn't care for the taste of Hook's clothes, and removes them delicately, noting their craftsmanship. Teeth can be tender; ask any nursing mother. Even a croc can undo an acorn button, loosen a waistcoat, slip off a boot without leaving a mark.

For all of these years, it's been Smee who has been keeping Hook in fine attire. And though Hook wasn't much for music, the whirr of the sewing machine brought him much comfort, sad comfort, on the Jolly Roger. In the back of his mind, the tug of a memory. A shadow, really. It was before the sea, before Peter, before aging Lost Boys started showing up on the deck with nowhere else to go. Long before all of that, there are two hands, stars. One holds a lantern. One checks his brow for fever. Sometimes, the figure lifts him. Sometimes, she whispers into his curls. Once, a kiss on the palm of his hand.

The croc removes the hook last. It drops into the lagoon without fanfare, while the other garments take their time, saturating on the surface, snagging on rocks and sticks. When the naked feast is fixed, the croc loses interest. Hook is only a man tumbled out of his ship. Where's the game in that? Leave him to the mermaids, the birds, the tide. Let time take care of what's left.

Twenty

To stave off the forgetting while in Neverland, Wendy quizzes her brothers about their past:

1. Write an essay of not less than forty words on *How I spent my last Holidays*, or *The Characters of Father and Mother compared*.
2. Describe Mother's laugh.
3. Describe Mother's party dress.
4. What color were Mother's eyes?

Blue. My sisters and I drag kitchen chairs together, make a ship. When I grip the spindles I notice they are dry, despite my dreams. We're not playing Peter Pan, exactly. None of us wants to be Wendy that way anymore. But our game is about orphans and oceans and the songs we sing bring us to real crocodile tears.

As we play, our father is riding a train home from the city. He has fallen asleep reading the *Times*, his head rests on the blurry window.

Our mother pushes a grocery cart at the IGA. She has folded her sweatshirt and placed it beside her purse in the child seat. Here, she makes a nest for the delicate tomatoes, the curved clutch of bananas. She doesn't trust the bag boy, never has.

When we are all together again, our shadows adjust. We part our hair into more flattering shapes. Our eyes shine darker, sea instead of sky. We are seven or ten or we are ever so much more than twenty, swallowed by time. We slip into our nightgowns, tie the waists of our robes, settle into our stories. Our home waits in the woods, in the dark. It is foolish to leave a light glowing outside our door. No one is missing. No one is expected or invited. It is foolish. But here's a moth wanting more. And here's a dream of a better, farther, light.

DONA NOBIS PACEM: A ROUND FOR FOUR VOICES

1. No Wine

They have no wine.

~the Virgin Mary, disappointed at a wedding

You were real, I suppose, but never to me. Who could refuse a mother in blue, hay in her hair? One who would shrug at a virgin pregnancy, concern herself little with the details of how, of who, content to just have her child, alive? God or no God, he was yours. That was enough to devote yourself entirely.

If you were a clue, you were easy to find. It was the Lord who was supposed to be everywhere, but there were six of you, placid in the picture window. Three of you topping a bookcase. You were made of glass on the VCR, flanked by wooden, gullible angels; and you were appliquéd on a wine-colored tapestry, faceless: a silhouette, moon-headed. Your likeness was a go-to gift for my mother, a sucker for clutter. But we never thought to gift her a Mary costume. Something well-dyed, with high thread count. A range of blues to wear over her hair, shoulders. Some ropey belt not too tight. Skirts appropriately hemmed so she could walk without tripping. In your robes, all might have been temperate. No dance with the thermostat. No double cardigans or desperate evenings where she stood in the snow in her nightgown. No bras hurried off in the living room whenever Jessica Fletcher was solving a bloodless murder in Cabot Cove.

At your shoulder, birds. At your feet, snakes. You were supposed to be crushing them with your heel, but they never looked dead. They might have been your friends. They might have fallen from under your skirts. The birds might have flown from there, too.

I am boxing you up with St. Francis of Assisi. I am boxing you up with a lampshade. I am boxing you up alone. Dad has had a stroke (*of genius!*) My mind says every time. The pamphlet at the rehab? Coping with a Stroke (*of genius!*). The email to my college bestie? We are all trying to find a new normal after my dad's stroke (*of genius!*). The Google search on whether it is wise to bring my dad into the swimming pool (Learning to swim after a stroke (*of genius!*)). So. Dad has had a stroke (*!*) and my parents are moving south. Closer to some of their children. Closer to me.

And all of you are coming, of course. She wouldn't leave you behind. But there is no room for you in the new apartment. Most Marys are bound for a storage unit. I may never see you again. Is there anything you want to say? To me? To one another?

In the Bible you only say a handful of things. To the angel announcing your virgin pregnancy, it's *May it be done to me*. To your sub-divine sister, you brag, *From now on, all generations will call me blessed*. You're not wrong. Years later, you scold Jesus when he disappears for three days at the Temple. He scolds you back. And at the wedding, maybe you're a little jealous because you never had one, at the wedding you complain, *They have no wine.* To silence you, your son performs his first miracle, casts a spell on the water. Did you drink it then? Did you trust it? Was it oaky, otherworldly, too dry? Did you tell him?

I imagined my siblings and I would crack open a bottle once the truck was packed and the house was empty. But we are too tired, too sad, and without a corkscrew, not to mention wine. The tap water, for years pristine and delicious, has grown questionable. The swimming pool? Empty. Filling with earth, the once-blue lining muted and torn into ghost shapes under the weight. The retaining wall is caving in. And still we say *miracle* as the sun sets behind the dumpster. We say *this house; we did it. We can't believe we did it.* Our words are knick-knacks—glossy, useless, nowhere to put them.

We sleep hard on the floor. Our bodies are everywhere.

You're going away forever, Mary. No angels, no sisters. No surly, holier-than-thou twelve-year-olds. No sober parties. The only word that works in a box is goodbye.

But let me say this, too. Blue is your color, girl.

Even in the dark.

2. The Astonishing
For Saint Christina Mirabilis (b. 1150, Belgium)

Your children were the children of God, and you gave them—your sisters, your neighbors—what they wanted. Proof. It should have been plenty, waking up at your own funeral, your body floating to the church rafters, the fires that lit you up for hours, until you grew bored of the horror and walked out of them, smoldering. What more could the doubting Thomases demand? An off-kilter sun in the Fatima sky? A crucifixion toasted into a ripple-style potato chip? The truth is, once God shows his cards, we are quick to dismiss miracle as madness, even malice. Twice, you were imprisoned when your holiness seemed too good to be true, too good to be good.

Eighth-grade Confirmation. I found you in one of our household *Dictionaries of Saints*. I wasn't sure about my faith, lit only by fear, but I was a sucker for sacraments. With Holy Orders off the table on account of my sex, and Baptism, Communion, and Penance under my belt, I was halfway to saved. Counting was something to count on: Ten Commandments, Fourteen Stations of the Cross, the Fifteen Mysteries of the Rosary—Glorious, Joyful, and Sorrowful, Lenten candles and Advent calendars, the tallying and exchange rate of venial sins in confession, my debt paid off in the pews, on my knees. Usually ten Hail Marys and one Apostles' Creed.

Catholic math aside, what charmed me about you, Christina, was the way you kept to the limbs of trees, far away from your believers. They say that you couldn't stand the smell—of people, of sin—that you climbed high every chance you got. Were you holding still up there, waiting for the people to make their way, or did you leap and swing, cut a new path, a medieval parkour course, a prayer in motion? The dictionary held no illustrations, but I imagined you in timeless rags, purples and grays. Something layered but easy to move in, something worn by a modern dancer modern dancing. So this was a way to snag a place in Heaven. Put on a show but run to the wings before the applause. Never collect your carnations. Stand in the freezing river for days, sure. They'll see you. Surrender to the wheel of the watermill, go round and round. They will hear the crush of bone but before they can touch you, you'll split. You'll head to the thatched roof, the blackjack pines. Anywhere above, away.

So I chose Christina as my Confirmation name. You were proof that this whole salvation thing was a bit suspect. While my classmates chose patron saints that had legible virtue—Lucy, martyred virgin; Francis, lover of poverty and birds—I enjoyed telling people that I had chosen to name myself after the patron saint of lunatics.

It was a lofty move, a soapbox in its own right. But I was

practicing being above it all. Earlier that spring, I'd been ousted by my group of girlfriends for some mysterious collection of middle school transgressions. My truest friend had been Karen, brilliant and bold. She had divorced parents, and this proximity to sin gave her certain authority. The previous year, she had volunteered the two of us to spruce up the classroom bulletin board. We covered it with pictures snipped from her mother's magazines, horrifying images of the genocide in Rwanda, not exactly what our teacher had in mind when he took down the previous month's life-explaining cell diagram—nucleus, mitochondria, endoplasmic reticulum.

Karen had a compassionate soul. She was also thirteen. So when our peripheral friends—the mean, skinny one; the heavy-lidded Irish step-dancer; the seemingly queer hockey player who said all of us were gay, her favorite insult—soured on me, Karen followed suit. The only real discord I can recall is a moment when Karen confessed that they were planning to try marijuana. I'm sure I gasped. I had, after all, won the D.A.R.E. essay contest in sixth grade. I could not believe that my actual friends would dare to smoke up, to get high.

They grew away from me and finally, one lunchtime, held in the classroom, one of them asked, *Doesn't it suck when someone you hate keeps sitting with you at lunch?* And Karen said, quietly but clearly, *Yeah. It does.*

It was easy to depart. My heart played dead, my sandwich seemed to repack itself into the aluminum foil I had just unfolded. I rose from the chair without snagging my long hair on a loose nail, and I floated across the room, to my desk, alone. A boy I liked—one I had called on the phone in the summer, one who had surely seen through but not questioned my highly rehearsed claim that such a phone call was no big deal because I was calling *every single person in our grade*—stood near me. *Why are you sitting alone?* he asked. I studied the foil and admitted, *I can't talk right now because I'm trying really hard not to cry. Okay,* he said cheerfully, and then he kept quiet but also kept eating his chips near me and not in a disgusting hungry boy way, but like a real person with an appropriate appetite, and I felt enormous gratitude to him for years after.

Even so, on the day of my Confirmation I could count my close friends on one hand, if that hand belonged to Saint Eurosia, whose hands were cut off before her beheading. Which is to say, I had no friends. I had my family. And I had you, Christina the Astonishing, cultivating your loneliness in a treetop. Taking your name felt like taking a dare, like casting a spell on myself. And if it took, good. And if it didn't, well, maybe also good.

Here's the truth: I was no good in trees. At twelve, I'm not sure if I had ever climbed one. Is it possible for a landscape to fail you? Is it possible that my house in the woods was circled by the wrong trees? Leggy birches or dense, sharp evergreens, none suitable for climbing? No, there were the two crabapples, at least. I could have gone up if I had tried to go up. One summer afternoon, I stood between them. Wary of yellow jackets but inspired by the Magnificent Seven U.S. Gymnastics Olympic team, I set out to master a handstand. I had no aspirations to be a gymnast. But the way I saw it, these girls, who were my age, excelled at childhood: flipping, flying, defying gravity. Kerri Strug on the vault, Shannon Miller on the beam, the Dominiques' floor routines on the bouncy blue, the ponytails, the crowd-pleasing *Devil Went Down to Georgia*.

I, on the other hand, floundered at youth. And so I practiced, flanked by the crabapples, their fruit already rotting. It didn't occur to me to use them for balance. Instead, I pushed my hands into the grass, hurled my legs into the sky with too much force, and landed flat on my back. I did this about a hundred times before I gave up. I don't remember feeling sore, just an acceptance that I was built for falling down, alone. It was my kind of sacrament, the kind that feels holy but can be worn out, forgotten, annulled. And, over time, it was.

And still, I sense that girl's longing when I show my boys how to float into a handstand in the summer yard. Show them to let their heels kiss the body of the dogwood for balance, that the tree won't dodge or disappoint. She's there; she tosses her halo up into the magnolia for Nolan and Silas to chase. Or there's a bird or a squirrel or some other sacred soul at work. And I am bound to follow them up. They go farther than I go, but I go.

The spell of your name, Christina, it hovers into my high school years. And one late night, I am in the woods with new friends. We sit on the earth; we are circled by trees. And we hold and believe one another's exaggerated stories, about the blessings and curses we know of the world. And no one wants to flee. We have cigarettes. We have lights to make them burn.

3. I Am Reaching Out Because

It is a sin to follow your horoscope because only God knows the future and He won't tell us. Also, we can tell horoscopes are false because according to astrology, Christ would have been a Capricorn and Capricorn people are cold, ambitious, and attracted to Scorpio and Virgo, and we know that Christ was warm, loving, and not attracted to anyone.

~Sister Mary Ignatius in *Sister Mary Ignatius Explains It All for You* by Christopher Durang

Dear Christine,

Hello! Are you the Christine H. that taught at Our Lady of Lourdes High School in Poughkeepsie, New York in the late '90s? If so, I'd love to hear from you.

Hi Christine,

Do you remember me? My name is different now. I used to be Marianne Upham, a name I shrugged off at marriage but began to miss a few years in. It seems too late to change it back. Like it's too late for me to get my belly button pierced. But I can still pierce my face or get a tattoo above my heart. I can still do things. What about you, did you marry? My journalist friend says you might be hard to track down because probably you married, lost your name.

If not, are you a jazz vocalist in Chicago? Or a teacher in the Buffalo public schools? You seem too young to be the glass artist in Tasmania. And it's hard to imagine you penning *Healthcare Price, Cost, and Utilization Benchmarks*, but lots of theater people end up in jobs they'd never imagine. Me, I wrote for a med tech company where everyone was young and hip and the vast stunning buildings were designed around stories people believed in— Alice in Wonderland, Harry Potter, Oz, Jules Verne, Grimm—and there was a waterfall and an adult slide plus organic food and all you had to do was work all of the time. I wrote about ambulatory software and cardiology workflows. I was bad at my job, bad at explaining.

Dear Ms. H,

Are you you? Did you direct the Christopher Durang play *Sister Mary Ignatius Explains It All For You* at my very Catholic High School? Was I Sister Mary Ignatius? Were you fired after one performance?

Did you know the high school used to be downtown, across from a crack house? That it was always winter? That my sister fell down the stairs there and was never the same?

But around the time that you arrived, the school moved to the old IBM headquarters. Lots of the kids' parents worked at the new IBM headquarters and maybe it changed how the parents felt towards their children, to drop them off at their old offices. Maybe everyone expected different things after that.

Dear Ms. H,

Were you Catholic? Or a bad teacher? Neither seems right, but why else would you teach at our school for so little compensation?

You know who wasn't fired? Mr. B., tenth grade English teacher and cross country coach. He said *Star Trek* was basically *Moby Dick*. He praised me when I ran so hard I threw up. When he thought an essay was bullshit, he would draw a bull, shitting, in the margin. Then staple a McDonald's application to your essay. I thought he was a good teacher. That's how much I didn't think about things then.

Dear Christine,

I'm in Buffalo, which means you could be nearby. But you've not responded to my email. Was it creepy that I said I hoped you were okay in the storm? Was it a transgression to imagine you losing power, or caught in a whiteout, a snowbank?

Instead of meeting up with you, I'm watching the Bills game on my sister's TV. Well, watching the empty field. Moments ago, a boy had a heart attack on the field. His name is Damar. He took a hit. Then he stood up. Then he collapsed. Now the field is empty. I read later that after this type of heart attack you have eight seconds before you lose oxygen flow to the brain. Which explains why he was able to, briefly, find his feet.

Dear Ms. H,

I've told a couple of people why I'm looking for you and both of them have their own stories of vanished teachers. One teacher directed a production of *Streetcar* and my friend played Blanche DuBois and when she was getting fitted for her costume, the teacher told the costume designer that she was to look *like a moth to a flame. A moth to a flame.* He was fired because he was gay was the rumor. He had warning, though, he could finish *Streetcar* first, and he made promotional posters for the show that said damning things like, *Betrayal!* which were supposed to look like they were describing the show but were really describing the school.

The other teacher was fired for I can't even remember, but my friend's parents were the type to call out injustice and they were disappointed that their son didn't follow suit. If you met him today, you'd think he would follow all the right kinds of suits. But he was like me, and like Blanche. None of us remember doing anything, just shrugging our shoulders when teachers walked out of the school at weird times of day, carrying getting-fired boxes. I mean, we didn't see them with the boxes, but I bet IBM had these kinds of boxes. And I'm sure these teachers had a few personal objects that they wouldn't leave languishing in the desk drawers that used to be theirs and used to be an IBM employee's and they needed to put them in something so they could carry them all at once, away.

Dear Christine,

I mean, I've also told everybody from high school that I'm looking for you. One person mixed you up with Ms. N, who also left in the middle of the year but for different reasons. With her, we sang appropriate songs, Dona Nobis Pacem, in rounds, on risers on the stage where they used to have corporate pep rallies. The stage was small and covered in red wall-to-wall carpeting.

I am a soprano. Are you a soprano?

Dear Christine,

I've thought about asking Ms. M, and it might come to that. She really liked me, I had evidence. Once, when presenting a project on Alfred Hitchcock, I screamed like Tippi Hedren in *The Birds*. I think maybe Stasia Buyes scotch-taped some paper birds to my shoulders and hair. I was a bit nervous about the scream. I remember my heart racing. But I screamed as loud as I had ever screamed, right in front of the classroom which used to be full of cubicles and Ms. M laughed until she cried. I knew, in that moment, that if another student had screamed that way she would have grown angry. There would have been consequences. Which is why I'm reluctant to approach her about you. I can see her being fiercely protective of the school's decision to fire a teacher who directs a play in which a hateful nun, me, murders a bunch of people because of a toxic version of Catholicism, which also happens to be the toxic version of Catholicism peddled by some at the school. Ms. M would be worried that helping me find you might be bad for the school but they already got the priest who touched all those kids and this really couldn't be half as bad and also I am not trying to write an exposé. I am only trying to write to you.

Dear Ms. H,

I suppose Ms. M and Sister Mary Ignatius had some things in common, although you can't trust memory. I'm getting this one wrong right now. And I know that I conflate Ms. M with Ms. B, the guidance counselor, whose name took me several days to recall, but who is also unforgettable. Somewhere along the way, Ms. B was the strongest proponent for a strict uniform code and to show her resolve, she had chosen to wear the uniform, too. For years. It was jarring to see a woman in her late fifties in the plaid pleated skirt, regulation shoes, oxford shirt, approved vest. A total power move, I see that now.

Did you know that I got an exemption from the uniform sweaters because they gave me eczema? That my mother had the school logo embroidered on two 100% cotton sweaters she got at Land's End? How that was a rare tenderness?

But the regulation skirts also gave me eczema and you can't have everything and so I just lived with that for years, the backs of my knees and thighs constantly inflamed, red, agonizingly itchy. You would think the rash might have been worse on one side or the other but the blotches were even, matched. They were twins, a set of wings or two halves of a beating, bothered, heart.

4. Eve Is Cold

I once wrote a poem about Eve from *Adam and Eve* and Jill from *Jack and Jill* and they were sisters. Or maybe mother and daughter. Or maybe lovers. They were starting a tribe was the point. I was nineteen. I was new to poetry. Okay.

The poem starts with Eve's long hair. It's not covering her breasts like in all the church art. Its hanging all the way down her back like my hair did at the time. It's hard to tell what's hair and what's shadows of hair, but there is a purpleness at work. On her head, she wears a crown. Not a crown like a queen. She's wearing the crown, the top of the skull, of another head. Jack's head. A crown she found *tumbling around* a hillside of children. Adam is nowhere. Cain and Abel have already done their worst.

She's going somewhere. The speaker of the poem says, *blood has an endless commute.* The speaker of the poem says, *the boy he has died and her mouth opens wide.* And you can't tell if she's about to scream in horror, or yawn, or pray, or eat. These are some of the things you can do with a mouth open wide, wearing someone else's skull as a hat.

There's a pail involved. It holds an entire ocean, all that salt.

Eve invents clothes. Gathers what the earth offers, weaves it all together to wear. Eve is not ashamed. Eve is cold. Jillian, grieving her brother, helps stitch. The speaker of the poem says, *forget irrigation* for some reason. The speaker of the poem says, *the child we've prepared isn't there.*

At dinner, Eve and Jillian *sample the snake and the wine and the cake.* Which means they have killed the snake, tasted the devil's knowledge, failed to learn anything new. It's all just nourishment.

Later, they climb a different hill. They do that part together. They haven't invented shoes yet. You can imagine their feet.

Then Jillian goes off on her own, to fetch whatever she feels like fetching. She is done with tumbling after.

As for Eve, she lets Jack's crown fall from her head and finds herself free from old stories. She takes another path.

I wanted to write an Eve essay. I wanted to sit with Eve in the real, ruined garden. To show her my poems, my breasts, my haircut, my husband, my two boys who have murdered, as of this writing, nothing in the name of God. I wanted to sit with Eve, but she left long ago for the woods. To make herself up again.

THE GIRL THE GIRLS PIECE TOGETHER

But he looked at her hands and saw they were real living hands.
     ~The Girl with No Hands by the Brothers Grimm

Hands.

The pears in the orchard have been numbered with ink. When the hungry runaway scales the stone wall, studies the branches, she takes a moment to choose. Number nineteen appears to be the largest. Number two hundred and forty, one of the ripest. She settles on this one here, a smudged forty-two, within reach of her mouth. She keeps her arms at her sides and lifts her chin, takes the first wet bite with the fruit still attached to the tree. It's not because she has no hands, although she has no hands, cut off by her own father to satisfy one of Grimm's demons. It's because she has seen other women reach for love this way. No timidity, no hint of shame in how much space and thirst wait in their throats. They drink a kiss down like it's a meal, like it's a song singing itself. She wants a world where there is nothing to savor, no separation, no doling out or holding back.

Belly full, the girl sleeps at the base of the tree, her true love. In the morning, the king comes to count the pears and she is found out. And he loves her, even if she is a thief, even if she will never chop his vegetables. She gets a man, a set of silver hands. She gets an orchard and a quill pen to maneuver with her teeth when she wants to tally up all that is hers. Eventually, one child, a boy. Her branch. She marks his lucky palms. One. Two.

Feet.

My great-grandmother carries her market basket in the bend of her elbow. She has chosen a roast and some tinned cherries for a pie. There are plenty of potatoes at home, plenty of greens. Still, it doesn't hurt to have a few extra French beans in the pantry. She reaches for the high shelf, takes one for her basket. Goes back for another and loses her balance, loses the second can, which strikes her foot. She feels foolish, like my sister would, apologizing to those who pass. Or angry, cursing the store for the arrangement, as I would have, a quiet tantrum in her head as she grabs what's left on the list, heads to the counter, pulls off one glove to dig for coins. But with the glove goes the anger, dissolving when the boy at the checkout tells her what she owes. It's exactly what she's already calculated herself, and yet it sounds like not enough at all for this bounty. *Thank you, Charlie,* she says, meaning, *This was a moment here, where pain sharpened attention, and you in that smock, Charlie, and the warmth of the coins, and the exact weight of my groceries, and yes this throbbing starting up in my foot now as the jolt ebbs away, this unremarkable exchange will surface in my imagination until the end of my very life.*

She doesn't register the blood in her boot until she's halfway home, thinking it is sweat. Like my son, she clocks alarm with damp hands and feet. A doorbell or a siren; their bodies respond the same.

The toe box darkens. Surely blood. And the heat in that foot won't subside. It's early autumn in Lynn, Massachusetts, but there is little sun. Every other part of her is chilled. It is a pleasant dissonance. She imagines her foot as a warm animal, and looks down every few steps, tracking the growing shape of the stain. How to get blood out of leather, she tries to remember. Peroxide, she supposes, but maybe Dorothy knows a better trick. By the time she gets to her door, she is limping with the pain. It takes some time to undo the boot, to pull it off. Blood on the bathroom tile. Ruined stocking. This is more difficult to remove because the silk is enmeshed with the wound. She cries out in pain when the threads finally release. In the tub, the cold water feels good. She admires the half-moon of the cut, a perfect stamp of the can. She admires how the running water can almost keep up with the blood, almost convince her there is no wound at all. There is swelling, a stitch of concern, but she takes care of it all—the foot, the floor, the boot, the supper. She doesn't tell her husband because, well, she doesn't tell her husband lots of things. When he notices, days later, he is tender with her. He kisses the bandage, the ankle. She laughs, offers up her other leg, lets him play there instead.

She doesn't visit the doctor until the pain is intolerable. So bad that it has rendered parts of the foot—the toes, the arch—numb. The color is wrong. The doctor can tell right away. It is, in fact, too late. The foot is dead. The leg is dying. They have to take it. My great-grandmother's response comes as a surprise to the doctor, and to herself. Julia Riley does not think of the blade of the saw; she does not worry that her husband will turn from her new body. She doesn't imagine the maimed unfortunates she's pitied, or mourn her neighborhood wanderings, or realize, with a start, that they'll have to move out of their walk-up. She doesn't think of her children. She thinks only of the leg, that it is hers. And she tells the doctor no. And so, she stamps her fate.

Stones.

For dinner, we will have chicken breasts doused with garlic powder, covered in drained and crushed pearl onions, then baked in a casserole with Uncle Ben's white rice, a can of Hunt's tomato sauce, and a tablespoon of sugar. When the meal is almost ready, my mother will turn on the broiler. The sugar will help the rice blacken, her favorite part. But when it's time to eat, she loses her appetite, moves to the couch in the TV room. She can't get comfortable. Something is happening in her body. At one point, my mouth is stuffed with sweet burnt rice and I see that she is on all fours, rocking and moaning the way I will when I am in labor. But my mother is not in labor. All seven of us have already been born, are in the kitchen, growing, filling our bellies with pieces of birds. The verdict—we learn when my father calls from the hospital—it's her gallbladder. She's away for a couple of nights and returns short one organ and with orders to eat low-fat meals as she recovers. Meals like the chicken, which we serve to her and one another, over and over for weeks. When she is feeling a bit better, she shows me what I think is a bottle of pills, gives it a little shake. But it's a bottle of stones, the ones that were lodged in her body. They are a wonder, and I don't blame her for keeping them on the windowsill over the kitchen sink for decades afterward. Because look what she made.

Years later, when her body acts up again, an ultrasound reveals that her stomach holds a collection of undigested pills. Capsules that never cracked open, that slid down her throat and settled into some quiet corner. My mother finds this hilarious. She's a human maraca! If you shake her, you might hear a song.

Girls.

In the 1934 Warner Bros. musical film *Dames*, Ruby Keeler stars as the chorus girl you love so much that one of her just isn't enough. *350 Ruby Keelers* is what the movie trailer promises, and indeed, there she is multiplying. Busby Berkeley's got every chorus girl wearing a Ruby Keeler mask. It's a dream sequence, Dick Powell's, and the Rubys can do little more than tip their heads from side to side in the dark. In another shot, they hold the skirts of their white gowns out to the sides, arranged on some elaborate architecture, but still their feet don't move. The Rubys are metronomes. The kinds of girls who hypnotize but don't know what to do with you once you're under their spell.

Powell, Ruby's love interest, sings, *I Only Have Eyes for You.* Now the Rubys sit on the huge soundstage, each girl perfectly circled by her gown arranged on the floor. When they stand, it is to bow to a man's imagination, and to show what is under their skirts. Why, pieces of Ruby of course. An earlobe, a bang, a tooth, a nostril. All together, they make up a photo of her face. She's the girl the girls piece together. And when you think you can't get any closer to Ruby, closer than this close-up made of the underskirts of hundreds of her offspring, the camera moves in. One single Ruby eye. And out of the pupil of the eye comes Ruby, the real Ruby, on some invisible elevator. Finally, she takes her place in a gilded frame, which becomes a mirror, and then a window into the train car where Ruby Keeler pretends to sleep on Dick Powell's shoulder, where Powell pretends to wake up whisper-singing. Keeler will kiss him, but only after he tips her chin up, to make a better line.

Cuts.

Walnut Grove, Minnesota. *Little House.* Ma Ingalls catches her leg on a stray piece of baling wire. Just a scratch. She cleans it, fashions a bread poultice, and ties it in place, forgets it while she sets to baking several blueberry pies for the neighboring town's church bazaar. The cut festers. And when her body grows damp and woozy, she assumes it's from the work of the pies. Scooping the flour, cutting the butter, rolling out the dough, and crimping the crust with her fingertips, all the way around. She's alone. Pa has taken the girls to the picnic grounds a day early, to camp out, to let Ma bake in peace. Far away, her girls swing on a rope in their nightgowns, land in a shallow pond. One of them is brave. One of them is not. Pa has a favorite. The girls' hands begin to blister. Back home, night falls. Rain falls, turns to storm. One of the cows gets loose. Ma hears her lowing, her bell clanging, between claps of thunder. The wound is hot to the touch now; she knows she is in danger. She staggers outside, drags her leg behind her. She gets ahold of the rope tied to the cow's neck but the animal won't budge. *Come on!* Ma pleads. She is soaked and sick and it's all too much. Her vision blurs, her hurt rings every bell in her body and she passes out in the rain.

After a commercial break, she comes to, comes inside, manages to stoke the fire, looks to the Good Book for guidance. And there it is. What to do when you're crawling on all fours in your night-gown: *And if thy hand offend thee, cut it off. It is better for thee to enter into life maimed, than having two hands to go into hell. And if thy foot offend thee, cut it off.* Ma makes it to the drawer, fishes out her biggest knife. Sets it on top of the Bible. She ties off the leg above the knee. She heats the blade in the fire, makes it clean and ready to cut. You believe in her. Your faith has never felt so sharp.

Pa gets wind that something isn't right at home. You watch him race the wagon back to the house, take those corners with haste. You see him push through the door to find Ma on the floor. You're ready for the blood, the lot of it, but by the next shot she's in bed, under blankets, no hint of how much of her is still intact. And even though you've seen this one, and you know she keeps both legs, that she only opens the wound to let the infection run, you forget every time. You think of her as the badass mother who cuts off her leg when she has to. All it takes is a nip of moonshine, a bobby pin pulled loose to embolden her. A blade and a way to hold it.

Years later, when Mary's gone blind and Laura's gone married and Albert's overcome his addiction to morphine, the series ends. The residents of Walnut Grove learn that the town is not theirs, is not for homesteading. Some East Coast business tycoon holds the deed to the land. They have to leave. And they do. But first, a protest. Dynamite, intended for the local mine, is nestled into the corners of their homes and shops. The families gather together as they would in worship. Now, a montage of sorrowful, stubborn faces. Now, a cut to a set of hands ready to pump the detonator. It only takes one push. And it feels holy, how they blow their prairie home to bits.

Hair.

The Barbie's blonde hair hangs all the way down to her pointed toes. When you take off her hot pink, off-the-shoulder minidress, you find a button between her shoulder blades. When you push it, the hair retracts into the head, the body. As much as you want. You can give her a bob, or a braid that won't break her neck with its weight. That's the memory, at least. Hours with this doll, Totally Hair Barbie. Hours wondering how exactly the hair fits into her head, her chest, her pelvis. Longing for some version of this, for the feeling of being stuffed that way, full with myself. A self I could brandish or bury on a whim. But when I look, I find there is no button, no way for Barbie to ungrow her locks. My memory is wrong. When I give her that bob, I do it with scissors.

It is an act of rebellion, I suppose, as I am forbidden from cutting my own long hair. It's not until I am eleven or twelve that my mother agrees to remove a few inches. The weight is hurting my neck, I tell her. It is true. It is also true my mother is easily swayed by anything vaguely medical. And so I stand shirtless in the bathroom. She sits on the toilet, scissors at my back. At the bottom of my ribcage, I feel the back of the blade grazing my skin. Three cuts and she's done. I leave my mother on the toilet to go look in my bedroom mirror, to savor the dizzy lightness of losing a piece of me, to swing my hair around like a girl in a shampoo commercial. My mother holds my hair, long and straight with baby curls still springing at the ends, and she wraps it in aluminum foil, keeps it.

Ink.

My niece Anna turns eighteen during the first summer of Covid. She's lost her prom and her graduation, but is allowed this ritual, as tattoo parlors have been given the green light to reopen in Buffalo. Her family has been waiting for her to come of age, so they can go together—my sister Kathryn, her husband Ed, and Anna's older sisters. The youngest sister, Maria, is eleven, too young to get ink. But she doesn't need it, already has what they came here for. They point to empty spaces on their limbs. Bicep, forearm, ankle. The family has endured much pain together. Secrets, wrecks, hospitals, entire seasons where it seemed nobody slept. It is something else to choose your hurt, to schedule it, to have a moment to brace yourselves together, to declare, *I'm ready*. They all get the same shape. It's an X, a set of crossed bars. An extra chromosome, which lit up their Maria years ago. Down Syndrome, one piece of her. My sister would say that it's the least remarkable thing about her daughter, but others often use it as a reason to denigrate or elevate, a sickness or a sacrament, both ways to distance themselves, and their own children, from difference, to locate themselves on a map of safety, or certainty. Where are they? Over here. The tattooed chromosome looks like a broken infinity. It looks like a ribbon fixed on a gift. When I ask Kathryn, new to ink, how bad it was, how much it hurt, she only says, *It was worth it*.

Later that summer, she sends Anna to college. Sends Maria to pandemic fifth grade at her own worn kitchen table. She sends me the start of a book she's writing in the wee hours. She's got more to name, to claim.

Brains.

Julia North is the protagonist of the 1977 novel, *Who Is Julia?* The story goes like this. Julia, a bombshell supermodel, is bombshelling along one day when she sees a child, Timmy, in the path of a streetcar. She saves him, and is struck herself, her body crushed.

Her brain, however, remains in perfect condition. Timmy's mother, homely housewife Mary Frances, drops dead from the shock, falls softly to the sidewalk, suffers not a bruise. When the two women are wheeled into the ER, there is only one science fiction option. Put Julia's alive brain into Mary Frances's capable body, so one of them can survive. And it is done.

I meet Julia North as an undergraduate philosophy major. She's referenced in a John Perry dialogue where another fictional thinker, Gretchen Weirob, contemplates identity theory with friends while reclining on her deathbed. As one does. The question: who survives? Julia or Mary Frances? Gretchen, who has, just the other day, turned down the very same body transplant procedure in favor of certain death, says it's Mary Frances who lives. It's her body, after all. Her shag haircut and root canals. Gretchen's friends disagree, conclude that it must be Julia. Julia's memories. Julia's personality. Julia's anguish when she looks in the mirror to find a short brunette who hasn't lost the baby weight. In the film version, Mary Frances's husband wants his wife's body back. He tries to force himself on her. She fights him off, breaks a picture frame—the couple's wedding photo—over his head. She rebuttons her blouse and helps tend to his wound. As one does. He apologizes. Calls her lady. Okay, then. Lady. He'll settle for less. *What about being a mother to Timmy? He doesn't know the difference.* And here may be the true test. Though her body knows she is a mother to the boy (who is, incidentally, far too old for the onesie and crib on the screen) her heart doesn't turn. She is, in fact, Julia North.

As a college student, it is easy to imagine waking up in some other body. It seems familiar. The night before I start undergrad, I break out in terrible acne for the first time in my life, and it stays for years. Who is that girl, bad at makeup, hiding behind her hair? Where has she come from? Over the course of the semester I find some peace with Locke, Hume, Putnam, Parfit, even when they imagine men as jaunty cobblers swapping bodies with princes, while the women are stricken, limbs lost, lights out. (Perry's Gretchen, it should be noted, dies in the room while the men are still talking, perhaps the most realistic part of the whole scenario.) I, for one, am charmed by the possibility that I am simply a brain in a vat. If I am a brain in a vat, the logic goes, I can't be a brain in a vat. Because what's a *brain* and what's a *vat* to a vat-brain? Meanwhile, my boys have been told something about the imprecise edges of their bodies. *Molecules, Mom,* says my nine-year-old. Molecules give them deniability when they torment one another. *I can't hit him, Mom. How can I? Too many molecules. I can't even get close.*

Lights.

The refrigerator smells horrible. Its only occupant—a small orange box of Arm & Hammer—has maxed out its capacity to absorb odor. The fridge is dark, has been broken for a number of years, but retains its place of prominence in the center of my childhood kitchen. All my mother wants is for the thing to be repaired. It's the perfect appliance. The shelves are sturdy; the drawers open and close without catching. The freezer is on the top, none of this bottom nonsense, ridiculous. But Ed Bailey's guy says it's an impossible job. And even if it were possible *(which, Mrs. Upham, it's not)*, you could get a brand-new fridge for half the cost. *This,* my mother tells me, *is a sin.*

I'm with her. Things should be fixable. Everything new is cheap and plastic. The world, hell, handbasket, I'm there. Even Bailey's isn't what it used to be. But there's still the matter of the empty fridge. She assures me it's fine. She has my old dorm fridge in the mudroom, perfectly adequate for her and Dad. She will not bring that one inside, refuses to send the broken-but-perfectly-good fridge to a landfill. But on this visit I keep forgetting. My body opens the fridge twenty times a day, out of habit, and I'm hit by the odor every time. Often, it triggers my gag reflex. *Oh, Marianne. You're so sensitive!* says my mother. And I am. I want the fridge to work. I want her to display her individual rice puddings like cold, well-lit trophies, not stack them in a corner where I once spilled Jell-O shots that wouldn't set. I want her pens full of ink and right where she left them, want her television loud enough, her well-read newspapers restored to their original folds with no struggle. I want Publishers Clearing House to knock on her door with a bouquet of balloons and say, *The time has come! After all of those prayers, Mrs. Upham, you've won ten million dollars!* And then Ed Bailey himself would present her with the oversized check, and take a look at that fridge which needs hardly any work at all, a new belt, new bulb. Why, he just happens to have one right here in his hand.

Instead, years pass. And then my siblings and I fill a dumpster, two dumpsters, with all the things she didn't have the heart to part with. My husband and brothers wheel the fridge through the house, out the door. We are so tight on space that we fill the fridge with other trash before we heave it up and over. We stack damp books inside, broken toys, a mildewed leotard I once wore in a dance recital. Somehow, we get the fridge in the dumpster. We are past the fill line. My brother-in-law climbs on top and jumps on all the trash, trying to compress it. We cheer him on. And though we are technically breaking the rule with the fridge in there, and pushing the limits of the fill line even after my brother-in-law's dance in work boots, we leave the house early the next morning, when it's still dark. We pray that the folks picking up this dumpster will be generous. We are on highways and airplanes, speeding away. And they take the dumpster; we hear no complaints. They take everything.

Wonder.

Vicki the robot fits in a box. When we meet her in the first episode of *Small Wonder*, the girl is dismembered. Her creator, Ted, has brought Vicki home from work in a suitcase. She's hairless, naked. Ted's ten-year-old son lifts her torso out, holds it in his arms like it's an intact baby. Later, Ted will assemble and dress her, give her a wig, tell her what to do. In the morning, in the kitchen, he presents the finished, walking, talking robot to his family. She's so convincing that he spins her around, fiddles open the back of her pinafore dress to show them her circuits, to put them at ease. Vicki doesn't mind. Ted lifts her hair straight off her head, asking his wife if she'd prefer a redhead. Joan can't bear to look. She is both impressed and embarrassed by her husband. Why the pinafore, Ted? It's 1985, Ted. And anyway, Vicki can't be the redhead because red-headedness is reserved for the snoopy neighbor kid, Harriet of the impossible bangs. This one peers through the family's windows at all the obvious moments. Like when the boy is getting dressed and he asks Vicki to turn the other way. She turns her head, only, like the *Exorcist* girl. Harriet hovers, in shock. She rubs her eyes with her fists. Meanwhile, the boy orders Vicki around, tells her to pick up his dirty clothes, says he might be in heaven. He keeps Vicki standing in his toy cabinet. Poor Vicki.

But the thing about Vicki? She is strong as hell. And, out of robot spite she takes every instruction literally, a regular Amelia Bedelia. Vicki does, in fact, resemble Amelia Bedelia. Except Amelia Bedelia never lifts 20 gallons of water over her head, never lifts a bed clean off the floor to retrieve a dropped coin, never punches a hole in the kitchen door just to show that the solid and whole, the perfect and useful, the prop of a family, means nothing to her. It is all so easy to ruin.

Words.

I know nothing of Greek tragedy when I am cast as a member of the Chorus in Euripides' *Hecuba* my first semester of college. Before long, I understand there will be no singing, no box steps in the background. It's not that kind of chorus. This Chorus, made up of the enslaved women of Troy, is the conscience, the bard, the pile of voices that you can let run together. You don't have to know our names or track us across the black box theater. Fix your eyes on any of us, you fix your eyes on all of us. Except the director tells me there's a catch. My role in the Chorus will be different. *They cut your tongue out,* she says, meaning the Greeks. *So you can't actually speak any of the lines.*

She tells me to say everything with my face. I still mark all of the Chorus lines in my script with a yellow highlighter. But when the cue comes, the only word I can think of is tongue. Tongue, tongue, tongue. A thing that has been taken from actual women. I am only in my mouth, trying to determine where it might have been cut, how far back. I get a panicky sensation like I won't be able to swallow and so I am not able to swallow and this renders my breath shallow. Up here in the throat, above the lungs. I am praised in rehearsals. The Greeks sacrifice Hecuba's daughter, then murder her son. The Chorus, in our gray-purple rags, we help her murder Polymestor's boys in retaliation. We hold down Polymestor while she gouges out his eyes. We relish the vengeance, though we know, as Trojans, we are doomed. While Polymestor had no warning of his own fate, he knows Hecuba's. She will take the form of a dog with bloodshot eyes. She will climb the mast of a ship and fall to her death, redden the sea with her blood. All of our blood. Hecuba spits the prophecy back. *Polymestor* can drown in the sea. *Polymestor,* with his empty sockets, can inherit her doom. *Fate is hard,* Euripides tells us. But Hecuba won't believe it is hers.

Hollows.

A few months postpartum with my first child, I call my friend Valerie and ask her why I still can't bear to have sex. *Well,* she says. *Your vagina just exploded.* I am grateful for this candor, when my birth books and midwives and vaginally intact friends rely on metaphors involving flowers, onions, and coral reefs. I want my body beautiful and wise, stoic and self-aware. But it simply feels wrecked, hurt, incapable of healing. In the weeks and months to come, I'm told my scar tissue is *heavy.* I'm told that the pain should be *over.*

I'm told that the next step on the ladder of interventions is to cut me open and sew me back together. A do-over. Just the thought feels like a violence. To top it off, *severe nipple trauma* from desperate nursing and pumping because I am bad at turning myself into milk. I'd like to trust my body's intelligence, but I don't. I cannot distinguish my baby's hungry cries from tired cries from my cries. I lose no baby weight until I get the stomach flu and then I lose it all. An entire year passes. My body is erratic. And maybe gaslighting me. I have no space for any body in my body. But my husband and I adapt. We find new permutations of ourselves. Because becoming a mother means rebooting my body. I need to locate my limbs, my heart, rearrange my pain.

Thirteen months in, my cycle returns. It's a shock, a clock I've forgotten. The returning estrogen is a kind of pixie dust. The heaviness goes, the pain unfolds. Once again I have made myself whole.

When I was a girl, I went on a hayride. Some kids wore costumes. I didn't. We piled onto the back of a truck in the center of the village. We passed Good Tidings, Star Video, Vinny's Deli, then picked up speed at the base of the hill on East Main. I felt the pickup, felt the press of the accelerator as if it were my own heart. Without a thought, I leapt off that truck, into the street. I don't know why. It wasn't fear or regret. I was not known to be impulsive. And time didn't slow. I didn't soar. There was no flight. Just departure. Then a girl with hands full of gravel, a knee gushing red. I came to my feet and found the sidewalk outside the Village Pharmacy. And at the end of that building was a little café. I can't recall the name, it lasted just a short time. But I walked inside and a waitress, she looked like a mother, showed me to the bathroom and told me to take my time. I did. No one came looking for me. No one noticed that I had disappeared. When I was done, she gave me a glass of water and had me sit on the brown leather stool with a clean white towel pressed to my knee, still bleeding. But the knee wasn't where the scar would settle. My hand was in far worse shape. Why didn't I show her my hand, torn open, brimming with glittering stones wet with blood? Rubies.

NO SUGAR

It was an awful lot of water and very little coffee.
~A Tree Grows in Brooklyn by Betty Smith

N ot everything that grows is good.
　　Take Johnny's drinking. Not so terrible when it's just the newlyweds, sharing a night shift as janitors at the elementary school. He wears his dancing shoes, she, her high-laced kid boots and a cherry wool fascinator. She saves bits of chalk from the wastebaskets. He dusts, then plays, the piano in the assembly room. The couple is charmed by the tiny chairs and desks, which make them feel grown up, though they are shy of twenty. They make love on the chintz-covered sofa in the teachers' lounge as they wait for coffee to boil on the hot plate. They drink it with condensed milk, and the sandwiches Katie has packed—bologna on rye. Most of Brooklyn is unlucky and asleep. Most would die for a taste of such ardor.

And Johnny drinks other things. Scotch. Beer. Katie tends to him. But when the baby comes, he is drunk somewhere else. And when another comes the following year, he grabs the bottle like it's the branch of the tree that will break his fall. His daughter learns that when he is drunk, most folks read him as sober—quiet and deliberate. When he is sober, he is loose, joyful, singing *Molly Malone* on his dark walk home from a stint as a singing waiter.

In the morning, coffee. For all of them, their rare indulgence. While Katie skimps on food and coal, saves pennies for a someday house, she doesn't blink when Francie lets her mug go to waste. The girl loves the taste but not as much as she loves the warmth, the smell. It's weak, but it's real. And with a lump of chicory in the pot to make it better, bitter, darker. Her ritual—to let it cool beside her in its own time, and then to pour it down the throat of the kitchen sink. Johnny balks, but Katie insists on the girl's right to waste something, to feel rich for a minute.

I'm nursing a lukewarm light roast at my neighborhood coffee shop, not grading the student essays stacked before me. For decades, coffee has always, for me, meant Francie and Katie. Reading the book as a child, I felt my own capacity to be a hard and practical mother, and I promised myself that if I was, I would allow my children coffee, whether they wanted it or not. It would be a thing they could point to when they wondered about my love. (Thus far, they care little for it.) I'm thinking of mother and daughter, and I go online to locate the exact scene where Francie dumps her share. Before I can find it, I find something better. The family name, which I have forgotten somehow. Nolan. My son's name. My son, who has been told that he is no one's namesake.

So he's named after all of them. Johnny, the talented dreamer, drinker.

Katie, once soft, pity lost on her.

Neely, hearty, impulsive.

And Francie, bright, tender, a story-maker.

All along I thought that I just liked the sound of the name, the almost-symmetry, the shape of the word in my mouth. But this.

The Nolans keep me up, keep me company. This favorite family of mine, newly fresh in my imagination. How many nights did I read that book by flashlight, trying to calm my fears? How many times did I weep, knowing that Francie was my dearest friend? How could I have forgotten what they called themselves when I say their shared name a thousand ways to my child? When I fill my kitchen with the scent of coffee every morning?

These days I take it with whole milk, no sugar, though for a time I drank it black, and then a stretch of foolishness, French vanilla from a machine in the school library. I had to learn it. My mother never touched it, and for my father only instant, with a teaspoon of sugar. Instant lacks true aroma, and if it gave him coffee breath, I wouldn't know. He wasn't close enough on those off-to-work mornings for me to notice, though at times the air held a trace of his Gillette Foamy or Old Spice Body Talc as he went from the kitchen to the porch to the still-dark world.

So we weren't a family who smoothed one another's messy morning hair or hugged without occasion or sipped hot beverages together. So we gulped cold, sweet things out of disposable cups we abandoned on bookcases, and ate entire columns of Pringles, alone, in front of the television. Who's to say that's not a home worthy of a story? But after Dad's stroke, at the rehab center, there is real coffee, endless coffee, Green Mountain Premium Something or Other and in this new place I drink it with my father by a window.

Dad requests *unleaded* at lunch and dinner. My first visit, it takes a minute to see that the sugar packets and little creamers are out of the question for his weakened hands. He takes it black, and I take a chance, making it sweet and light for him without a word. I lift the cling wrap from the yellow wedge of cake that has gone untouched. He thanks me, digs in. Had he been hoping I would do these things for him, or has he learned to take whatever he can and not worry too much about what's left or what's next? Is this plenty?

He tells me about Felix—the name he has given to the left side of his body, the weak and uncooperative side. If he remembers his Latin, and he does, he knows the name means lucky, happy. Maybe not terribly lucky, but lucky enough. He talks to Felix in physical therapy. Leg extensions from the wheelchair. Short walks on the arm of some pretty-enough therapist. *Come on, Felix*, he calls to the foot that forgets. *Let's go, Felix*! I chime in. When have I cheered for my father before today? When has he heard me do so? When he got his master's diploma, that crowded auditorium, those itchy tights. Or those evenings he schooled the *Jeopardy!* contestants from the recliner; and that time when he beat my sister in a race on the beach, shirtless, barefoot in those orange swim trunks, his pride at such a thing too big, but I fed it, whooped and hollered like a child from some other generation.

Mostly, I called to him at night. He slept across the hall from us, would fall asleep with no trouble. And because I was too old to be scared, and too scared to put my bare feet on the floor swirling with demons, I called out to him, *Goodnight, Dad!* as if he hadn't been asleep for an hour, or two, as if this were just my regular evening John-Boy. And it could take a few tries. My sisters would grumble beside me, kick their blankets off, turn away, but he would eventually answer, and never with anger, *Okay! Goodnight, now.*

Even so, sleep couldn't beat my growing anxiety. Out came a book, a burning-out flashlight. On the cover, Francie, in sepia, lit by candlelight. Swirling cursive. I can smell the old pages. I can remember the exact weight, how I kept cracking the spine. It took two hands to keep open—one of those too-fat and too-narrow paperbacks, the print tiny, the pages prone to loosening themselves like maple leaves, so self-assured in their worth they could reject the order they'd inherited.

And what did I keep, after all? Not the arcs or the hurts, not the finely timed departures. I kept the coffee, the forgiveness, the mounting hunger for all kinds of nourishment, sweet and bitter, right and wrong. I kept the song, the name.

Dad's mother was a drinker. That's what my aunt says. My father doesn't remember, and doesn't deny it. He seems wistful for his child mind that could come of age and never have to notice. What he remembers is Mary Riley sitting with a perpetual cup of tea, her little afternoon pick-me-up. What he remembers is that she served the same to a series of neighborhood women who wept at her kitchen table. That she knew how to listen, how to be a woman steeped in anybody's heartache. None of it better or worse.

She would have been a friend to someone like Katie Nolan, doomed to love a drunk, raw-knuckled from scrubbing tenement stairwells, pregnant again, aware that her love for her children is uneven, unremarkable, addictive, irreversible. My grandmother would have shooed my father away, *Time to go, Paul.* She would have taken Katie's hand. Not one for metaphor, she would have ignored the tree outside, wrestling its way out of the sour earth. She would have closed the curtains, cut and sewn from a worn day dress, and put the kettle on. She'd find a heel of rye, maybe some bologna or a wedge of cheese, a few shortbreads. She'd tell Katie to stay as long as she needs, to keep her heart warm. To tend the forever loneliness with whatever she can reach. No need to make sense of life, to make believe it means something more. Let the Lord sort it out when the time comes. He could afford to do a little more around here, to tell the truth.

GIVE US ALL THE ANGELS

I t is late summer, a Tuesday, when I wake up and think, today is the day I will hold a dead baby. I'm wrong. It takes my sister's body until Wednesday to let her baby go. Give a mother a potion to coax out a baby who can't survive Earth and you'll see just how feeble potions can be. But eventually, there is birth. It coincides with death. And I am there. I hold my sister and I hold her daughter and I let the worst nurse on the scene, the one who was never within reach, the one who couldn't find enough pillows or towels or popsicles, I let her hold me when I lose it in the hallway.

I don't think about you, distant friend, until late that evening, in my boys' bedroom. They share it, tonight, with my sister's other daughter, healthy daughter, alive daughter, three years old, staying over a couple of nights while her parents bring her sister to Heaven. My boys are asleep and little Libby is almost there. She wants me to hold her hand to help her over the edge. I kneel beside her makeshift bed—crib mattress on the floor—and oblige. Her hand feels substantial. All three children seem enormous. My boys have kicked off their blankets, sturdy enough to stay warm on their own. Libby's stuffed owl waits on the pillow, unhugged. Such vigor, self-sufficiency. Given where I have just been it seems almost grotesque. The children breathe, scratch their bellies, reach into the darkness for sippy cups, flip their pillows for relief from their own relentless warmth.

Friend, I think of you. The baby that claps in your dreams but refuses the limits of any awake body. I think of the potions, the workshops, the needles, the herbs, the prayers that you have lived with year after year. Life so close it seems to glow on the horizon.

My older boy has turned blue, twice. A fever and seizure on his second birthday. And then, in second grade, a case of croup that leaves him suddenly big-eyed, gulping cold air, bent over the freezer. Lips blue, then limbs. It takes only seconds. My husband appears, heaves his dead weight off of the floor and they are gone, the hospital less than a mile away. I call a friend, speak nonsense until she gleans I need a ride. I wake my younger son, carry him downstairs, his warm little arms and legs wrapped around me. He's so light, so full of breath. It is easy to do the mundane—get him to the bathroom, help him with his shoes—I even pack water and slices of bright, dried mango. I think, maybe this is how it will be now. Maybe I will never again say, *this is to share with your brother*. I can't reach Rob on his phone and my friend arrives before I feel ready. But I walk out into the dark, buckle Silas into the car seat of another kid.

Nolan is almost whole when we get there. The doctor is giving him a special vapor to open his airway. The mask gives him too much anxiety, so she just holds the tube near his mouth, an offering. The vapor is visible, made of ghosts. It goes where it wants, frames his little face. *Nolan*, I say. *Nolan*. As if hearing his name will remind him how to inhale. I stand by his feet so I'm out of the doctor's way, I hold them as if they are the strings of balloons bound for the sky. His color is returning from someplace far away.

Hours later, when we have skirted the Heliox and the ICU, we blink, bored of hospital cartoons and pudding. At some point, Rob tells me about the impossible drive. Nolan terribly slumped, calm, whispering that there are flying machines in the streetlights. Rob carries him to the door and Nolan is heavy, Nolan weighs everything, his every breath a difficult pull. Before they enter, an old man who appears to be homeless materializes. Gives my son the sign of the cross, then wanders away. God, give us all the angels.

It's almost enough to send me running back to church, this gratitude. It's almost enough to just send me running. It's too much, this love. It grows but never grows old. It buckles me when I am bored. Waiting for school to let out, and then that parade of little backpacks. Or when I dig a garden bed for Early Girl tomatoes while my boys fill kitchen pots with the backyard, clover and sticks and hose water, saying *We're making you something.* Or when I board an airplane with so many bodies and we settle in like we are really part of something. And a voice says that a breathing mask will drop down when we need it. In the front of the plane, a flight attendant holds one in her hand so we will recognize it when it happens. She puts it on partway but not enough to smudge her lipstick. Takes it off. We take off, expecting to survive the journey. We believe we will return.

You tell me about one of your workshops. One that links infertility to a personality problem. One that suggests that if you get more creative in your art, more productive in your work, you might become more fertile overall. The facilitator likes to push buttons, bring desperate would-be mothers to tears. *It's so difficult,* you tell me. *But really amazing.* At one point, the facilitator singles you out, gets in your face, asks you, *Why do you think you should be a mother?* You don't have the right answer, any answer. You fall apart. *It's really amazing,* you say again. I affirm and affirm but what I'd like to do is find this person making money off of your pain and tell her to find her seat. That nobody gets to ask you such a question. That you have asked every question already and been met with only silence.

It's not for me to say what my sister's loss was like, or even what her tiny daughter felt like in my arms. Only that I wish this brink on nobody. I can tell you that as closely as we hold someone, we are still only near them. I can tell you the baby's name. *Elisha.* I can tell you that my sister called her name as she was being born. *Elisha.* Knowing that she would die the second she arrived. I called Silas' name when I was in labor with him. I called Nolan's name when he dropped to the floor on that terrible night. But now I get to say their names and it is easy, joking, stern, disappointed, doting. I've said their names eleven ways this morning. And every time, they hear me, turn their heads, meet my gaze.

There is a name for her, this child you long for. I hope you say it aloud. That your husband hears it. That your two pups know it, that they rush to the front door when you say it, ready for her to barrel through with her wide messy braids and little backpack. I hope that one day you don't see her coming, and she lingers out-side, rings the doorbell with her elbow. Her hands are full with her science project. A bobcat diorama she brandishes like a birthday cake. Lightly, she kicks the door with her light-up sneakers. They light up. The dogs run to the kitchen, the playroom. They come back, panting. You open the door and welcome her. You take the habitat from her hands. You and your husband helped her with it last week, but not too much. You're not the kind of parents that take over. You're not the kind that need everything to be perfect. When she decided, halfway through, that she wanted her bobcat hunting in the daytime, even though the library books say that the creature is nocturnal, you said sure. You helped her find the right color construction paper to make a brilliant sun to glue onto the night sky already underway. You told her, *Sweet girl, I bet that when a bobcat is hungry, they don't care about the time. They go searching at all hours, all over the hills.*

BLUEBERRY HILL

But it was Little Bear's mother instead. She was tramping along,
eating berries, and thinking about storing up food for the winter.
Little Sal tramped right along behind.
                              ~*Blueberries for Sal* by Robert McCloskey

, too, have lost my child in bear country. Show me a mother
who hasn't.

I, too, have felt fear grow legs, gallop through me, snap my sternum. Have run to any thicket that could hide a child and her empty
pail. When you run, you could run faster. But you suspect your direction
is wrong. And you sense she is beyond saving, anyway. In the clutch of
some paw. Choking on berries. Tangled in briars, her overalls all over.

But then there she is in the clearance racks, the tunnel slide, the
kitchen cupboard. She is no crow, no partridge. And it turns out you
weren't running. It hadn't come to that. You just stopped your air to
kill time. Made your feet fast but kept your bucket level. Running
would have said, *I picked this.*

What's remarkable is the ease with which Little Bear took her
place. You were certain it was Sal back there. The hint of warmth and

movement at your back. Some breath. The way her weight on the ground seemed to crumble the trail underfoot. Under the dirt, lungs.

Or were you plotting new space between mother and daughter? Had you lengthened your stride, skipped the best berries just to ease up her gravity? Just to swing your bucket with abandon, a circle to yourself on Blueberry Hill? Before your arms were weary of pick, carry, keep, save? Before lose or raise? If so, a snapped twig in your wake would suffice. A rough breath would pass in and out unquestioned. You were thinking about canning, if you were thinking at all.

The first time I picked blueberries I was three months a mother. My boy wouldn't start solids for three more. Solids? It seemed nothing would be solid again. I didn't even think to bring a container. I wasn't a container kind of person. The hill was flat. The sun was hot. The dirt was dust but the berries were ripe. They were good because they had to be good. To be blue was in their nature, too.

The berries were for me, as yours were for you. An elevation circled on a map. If I was holding fruit. If it was four o'clock. If I'd made a purchase. If I'd answered the phone. If we'd opened our windows. If our faces were soft. If winter was coming. Then. If. Then.

I have never said to my own mother, *I wish you lost me in a wild place*, but it is true. I imagined it often. The thrill, the danger, the way I'd indulge in the berries until it was time to ration them, build a fire, sew fallen leaves into blankets and dresses and baskets. But mostly I dreamed of reunion. Hollowed by my absence, she would, at the sight of me, fill to a new brim. She would keep a quiet wonder, like you. She wouldn't shout my name, too lucky she would feel, seeing me when I thought I was unseen. No worry would grow in me. But I would know to turn. She would look part bird and, with the pines far behind her, so small she could trample them, part bear.

My boys don't know about the days I am early for preschool pick-up, watching them on the playground, free of me. They don't know that I linger outside their bedroom door to hear their chatter as they fall asleep. That I weep when they make it up another branch in our magnolia. Or when they meet you, and Sal, and love you like I do.

At my mother's, the boys are joyful in the clutter, but the house can't hold much more. The shades are drawn, old books and newspapers stacked high. I forget which story is mine when we are with her. When I try to contain their play, she clucks that boys will be boys. When I let their voices soar, she retreats to the kitchen. She prepares her first meal of the day, mid-afternoon. A bowl of Kellogg's. At the counter, her back rounded from so much carrying, she counts the blueberries left in the pint. This is her rare indulgence, paying for fresh in winter. And she is choosy. She holds them in her hands like they are lucky coins, happy with their ripe weight. When she pinches them, they surrender just enough, just barely, no harm. She washes them well, lays them on paper towels, likes them damp, not dripping. Arranges them in such a way that the pouring of milk will not disturb a single one. My boys destroy her living room or play perfectly, eyes shining, dimples working, and she looks away, feeds herself without apology. I leave them to sit with her.

When you were out there, just you and Sal and the ragged fertile hill, you meant to pick more berries. What you managed in the end would never, it seemed, get you through the fallow months. One cold snap and they'd be used up. A couple of pies, maybe. One blueberry glaze on a roast. But still you carried the pails into the kitchen, and began the work of putting up. Sal climbed a chair, to even your heights, to see the abundance. And, in the end, you filled every jar you could find. You filled every winter.

THE TAKING
BOY

And the tree was happy.

~ *The Giving Tree* by Shel Silverstein

M y friend Kristen says the book should be called *The Taking Boy*, a story of using mothers up. A story of hollow children, taking our apples to sell, our branches to build, our trunks to carve into boats that will float them away. A story that grows a boy into a bitter old man, leaves a mother stumped. Kristen and I have two kids apiece and they have climbed our trunks and whispered wishes into our hair and demanded impossible gifts with no shame. We're power walking at work, past the quad, behind the practice fields. Late fall. I have nineteen minutes until my next meeting. She is three thousand steps behind where her Fitbit wants her to be. We've talked tantrums and grant applications, committee work and gifted education, and she asks me, *Do you think we're missing the point?* It's the kind of question that should stop us in our tracks, invite us to take an extra breath of cold, bright air. But we don't have time to stop. That's what the walk is for. A stop that's not a stop. *Probably,* I answer, moving, staying warm, missing lots of things.

The book—its sketches and sadness—means little to me, a mere shower gift years back. But it makes me cry, and my boys like that. And the man is stupid, they like that, too. *A single crop of apples won't get you that much money,* they say. *What kind of house can he build with those branches? What kind of boat?* And they say you, tree, are equally dumb. A mother should know to stop giving. This boy will keep taking until there is nothing left. It's how boys are built.

You must, therefore, be a bad mother. Blame me for this idea. I was explaining some consequence for rude behavior. *If I let you (talk to me that way / leave crumbs all over the floor / pee on your brother), I wouldn't be a very good mama, would I?* They were quiet for a moment. Their faces flush with realization. I don't think it had ever occurred to them that mothers could be good or bad. That parents could be better or worse. And now it will never un-occur to them. *No,* they said. *If you let us (decapitate the stuffed animals / have candy for breakfast / wear these stained pants on picture day), you would be a bad mama. A bad one.*

My older child has recently learned that a mother might be bad not only through neglect or overindulgence but through outright abuse. He knows that some parents harm their children. That some grown-ups have mean ideas, wild hands, ways to hurt that are hard to imagine. He wants these grown-ups dead, he says. And in prison. He wants to gun them with a knife and kick all of their horrible arms together until the glue dries and they have to stop. Until the pain they make is contained and returned, a gift in a box. I want him in a tree, away from all of that.

But a bad mother is not the same as a sad mother. You are sad, despite the book's refrain that the boy makes you happy, eating your fruit. Makes you happy, weaving crowns out of your leaves, happy, carving initials into your bark, cutting, chopping until your branches fall from their space in the sky and crash to the earth, that ragged sketch.

Here is more of me, mothers say. Mothers smile, not enough, too much. There is no hiding from my boys how pleased I am with their rendition of childhood, when they like art and vegetables and climbing, when they roll their eyes at Tough Guy t-shirts and yogurt tubes decorated with cartoon characters. *Mom, it's not like Spiderman is in that yogurt, right? The yogurt companies just want kids to whine to their moms until they buy junk.* And I hug them close as if they are the most brilliant children on the planet. And I worry at times. Have I made them feel that my happiness is their responsibility? Or that my joy is theirs alone to harvest?

And apples fall, but not far. I am the child of an unhappy mother. Unhappy despite the fact that not one of her seven children was using drugs, failing school, running away, leaving the church or coming out of the closet. Yet. We slouched, spoke with the wrong voices, insisted on catching our death with damp hair and bare legs though the weather demanded tights. It's not that we didn't try. To make her happy, I went a decade without a haircut. I prayed to St. Theresa on my knees every night of third grade. I volunteered to go grocery shopping with her, arranged fake flowers—tulips, carnations—on the bathroom counter, hand-copied choreography for her Adult Tap students, countless index cards with the perfect words—*shuffle, hop, step, slap, dig, stamp, triplet, around the world, drawbacks, scuff,* and *Maxie Ford.*

It wasn't until I was seventeen that I realized I had no business making her happy. It happened all at once. Her eyes were on the news—fires, kidnappings, events she blamed on those taken—and I was leaving the living room, exasperated. And suddenly, I wasn't. *Good night,* I said. *I love you,* I said, meaning it. It was as if a seed I never saw planted now sprouted, flourished, found itself radiating years of sunlight it had been secretly hoarding. Let me be clear. This wasn't understanding or forgiveness. This wasn't some generous bouquet gripped in a fist. She knew; she didn't meet my eyes when I said it. This was a gift to myself alone. I could be a tree and be alive. I could be a tree and not be locked in place, in wanting. She was my mother. She was only my mother.

I am sad from time to time. The Taking Boy is sad, too. He never gets his money, his house, his wife and children. Or if he does he loses them somehow. Maybe he is bad to them like he was bad to you. Maybe they give him away. Maybe his sons say, *We're the boy, now. You have to be the tree!* and he isn't able to feed them or hide them or hold them to the brilliant sky. I don't blame the boy. And I don't blame you, tree. When I was pregnant with my first, my mother's womb held cancer. When I visited, she was sick from chemo, the news was on mute. And I told her, a baby. To make her happy. But also because I wanted something in return, a gift. I wanted her to tell me that I could be good at this lovely, lonely give and take. That I could be good. Who else could make me believe a thing like that?

RELENTLESS HEALING

I'm not a lady. I'm a doctor.
~Dr. Michaela Quinn, *Dr. Quinn, Medicine Woman*

The doctor can set a boy's broken leg. She can soften the blacksmith's lumbago and she can improvise a tracheotomy. Now she douses a clean rag in chloroform, muffles a birthing mother's pain, cuts her belly to save the trapped baby. She heats a needle with a candle, worries a thread through the eye, stitches the mother back together. The doctor listens to the shop keep's heart when it beats wrong, presses a packet of powder—digitalis—into her palm. Tells her to take a pinch when she needs to slow it down. The patient stows it in the pocket of her apron, where her husband's hands no longer wander. Used to be he would come up behind her when she filled the gumdrop jar, ask the price of something sweet. It was a nod towards later, towards tomorrow, towards the future, when the sewing notions arrive from Denver, and the tinned cherries are perfectly stacked, and the new sacks of grain are sliced open and staged with clean, gleaming scoops.

The doctor, Michaela Quinn, from Boston, pulls wax from

Horace's ear. She pulls a bullet from Chief Black Kettle's neck. She does all this and more in the first episode, but it's not enough. Because she can't be a man, be what the townsfolk expected when they heard a doctor was coming to the frontier. And she can't be a pioneer woman. She's never ridden a horse or swept a floor. She rents a room, honest to goodness, in the boardinghouse, unheard of for her sex. Worse, she has no prospects and no desire to be a mother. When Widow Charlotte is on her deathbed—snake bite— she begs the helpless doctor to raise her three children. Michaela answers, *Not me*, but of course she relents. It's an old-timey deathbed and a TV pilot, after all. But there's no unsaying those words, no untangling that refusal from every embrace she offers the children in the six seasons and decades of syndication to come.

Michaela tries to fill the role of mother, as one fills a basin with water or a syringe with morphine. She can be liquid, like when she has the barber pull her tooth—a perfectly healthy molar—to show her grit. And without a pull of whiskey. But she has no such bearing with the children. When little Brian knocks over the candy jar at the general store, she's too harsh. She shatters his heart. He shouts, *I hate you!* And he's the sweet one.

Michaela—Dr. Mike or Dr. Quinn but you like Dr. Mike—she wants to make it up to him, to all of them. She buries her hands in dough, kneads it wrong. And the bread burns but at least now there is flour on her face. At least now there is proof of a domestic afternoon.

/   ~

Mom! Are they ready yet?

On the commercial break, from somewhere, a boy calls to his mother. She's in the kitchen, calls back, *I'm still working on it. These things take time!* If the boy would ever step into the kitchen, which he won't, he would see that the easy-to-make Rice Krispies Treats have already been made, cooled, and cut. The mother, in fact, is eating one right now, stretching out the marshmallowness, stretching out this time so she can savor the sweet, the solitude, and also the book in her hands, *Tender Secrets*. It has a pink cover. A bird and a rose in bloom. It's for ladies. You are saving this up in your mind for the future. How unlonely this mother is when she is alone. After a particularly thrilling passage, she closes the book and gets ready for her family. She messes her '90s hair. She dusts flour on her face and dips her fingertips in the fishbowl to spritz herself, fake sweat. She adopts a weary posture and lets out a theatrical sigh as she carries the platter through the swinging door. The voiceover (male, folksy, sanctioning her ruse) says these treats are so good that *Your family will think you slaved over 'em. All afternoon.* And he's right. The husband says something about *knocking yourself out.* The kids say *Mom!* like kids never say *Mom.* Like they are nearly scandalized by how much of herself she put into this dessert. Who knows how many kids are through those doors. It doesn't matter. She's already fed herself.

/   ~

Here is the snake and here is the stick. They've been friendly for centuries. One alive. One formerly alive. One curving, seeking. One fixed, no nonsense. Here they are on the cover of a thick blue book in a dimly lit hallway in a single-story ranch. Your single-story ranch. There could have been a second story. The basement is enormous, a full shadow of the house itself. Its only use is accumulation. When the church gets new pews, a few of the old ones come here. When the metal high chair pinches its last baby finger, here, to rust. When the cabinets, when the books, when the thrift shop, when the costumes, when the swing set, when the mattress, when the hatbox, when the dolls. When a jar of pennies crashes to the floor, the mess remains for years, coins and shards, tender and danger. Because there are mice here, too. Because they could carry a virus that fills the lungs if you stir up the dirt where they've been, if you sweep. Your family is the catching kind.

And so you find the spine of this blue book—*The American Medical Association Family Medical Guide*—more than you find the Bible. You are seven children in total and your mother is a pessimistic part-time nurse. There is no shortage of symptoms in this house. Etched into the book's hardcover, the symbol of the snake winding around the stick. This is the Staff of Asclepius, the ancient Greek god of medicine. The story goes that one day, Asclepius is out for a walk and accidentally impales and kills a snake with his walking stick, as ambling Greek gods are wont to do. Well along comes another snake, mouth stuffed with herbs. The alive snake presses his leafy mouth to that of the dead snake and now both snakes slither. Asclepius is not too arrogant to learn from a beast on its belly. And it just so happens that he's got a dead friend needing revival. So he finds the same herbs and now he plays the role of doctor. He brings the dead back to life. And the snake, sometimes a symbol of poison, becomes one of promise. One that graces the emblems of apothecaries, hospitals, and insurance claims for years to come. A symbol that survives the Middle Ages and your slightly hypochondriac childhood. It means healing.

/   ~

The Cheyenne tea is made from purple coneflowers. Half the town has the flu, the stagecoaches won't come through until the epidemic has passed, and Dr. Mike is out of quinine. But still she refuses to offer her patients the tea. She doesn't know the proper dosage, says she can't trust a medicine with which she's not familiar. Sully, her love interest, a white man with a tragic past and a pet wolf, a white man who keeps company with the tribe and is known to announce his arrival by throwing a tomahawk in Michaela's general direction, is disappointed. For a rebel, she's far too faithful to the rules of medicine.

When Dr. Mike herself falls ill, of course it's this tea that will save her. But instead of bringing her a cup, Sully throws her fevered body up on his horse, gallops off to Cheyenne territory, to Cloud Dancing, who has a fire going, who is ready to perform a ritual of healing. Presumably, Cloud Dancing doesn't catch the virus. Presumably, the Cheyenne stay healthy because of their mystical nature-wise ways or maybe because they are not welcome in town, the site of contagion.

Colleen, one of Dr. Mike's new children, stays healthy, too, though she insists on being in the thick of it. She serves as a nurse for the quarantined, who are lined up in beds in the old boarding-house. Colleen hovers over sweating, stinking bodies. She wets a rag, presses it to a forehead, cheek, chest. The postman staggers in. So does the barber. The Reverend kneels bedside, clutches his crucifix, closes his neighbors' eyelids when their breath stops. Others feel called to help, too. Emily, whose baby has just pulled through. Myra, a saloon girl, tender to a fault. There is intimacy in shared illness. And even as the folk mourn and fever-dream, they take some comfort in undergoing such difficulty together, in the damp bedding, the endless sweat, the wheeze in their lungs. When Colleen brings a drink, they drink without question. They are grateful for any offer, any taste.

/   ~

If summer had a taste, it would taste colorful as a celebration, excited as a kid, and welcome as a breeze. Like the latest Lemon Berry Sippers from Country Time. Only it's spelled *Lem'n Berry.* Maybe the missing *o* in *Lem'n* is the lemon. And the lemon has already been picked.

You're at a parade. This is America. You can tell because everybody is waving. Waving is a prime symptom of America. And a white dog wears a red handkerchief around its neck. And a grandfather carries his granddaughter on his shoulders. And another child carries a pinwheel past an American flag, a police officer, a cloud of confetti. An antique car rolls by, unhurried, same as the three members of the marching band, who do not play their instruments, because of the waving. Almost everybody is white, but up on a veranda, a young Black girl stands alone with her beverage. The camera lingers and we hear the voiceover, maybe the same voiceover from the Rice Krispies Treats ad. He says that Country Time is *making the taste of good old-fashioned lemonade brand new.* Close up on a bowl of berries, rinsed clean in a sink. You can't see who rinses the berries. But if they're rinsing the berries they are missing the parade. And that means you're missing the parade. At least part of it. But that's how it goes with parades. You can only witness the parts that you witness.

/   ~

Sully is not welcome here. He is trespassing, planning to sneak a sample of water from Harding's Mill. Folks in town are falling ill and Willow Creek is suspect. Dr. Mike is here, too, against Sully's wishes. For all of his earthy clothes and enlightened one-liners and self-righteous bursting through of saloon doors to save women, he still scorns them. He warns her, *Please don't be using that fancy soap because if I can smell it then everybody else can, too.* He's annoyed at all of her frivolous lady things. *Junk,* Sully says, of the hairbrush and mirror tucked in the bag with the test tubes.

Widow Charlotte has been dead for six episodes and that's a sufficient interlude to allow for another rattlesnake. This time it goes for Sully. But just when it's ready to strike, Michaela uses her mirror to catch the sunlight, to blind the snake, saving Sully from certain death. *Handy little piece of junk, huh?* She deserves to gloat but it is unbecoming. To Sully. To you.

The water is tainted all right. Harding uses mercury to pull gold from ore and dumps the wastewater right into the creek. When he finds Michaela and Sully, he plans to dispose of them, too. But then his own son, a babyface wannabe tough guy, gets sick from moonshine made from the creek. He feels it in his belly, his tender gums, his teeth, his hair. He's withering, a far cry from his posture just a few days prior outside the saloon. There he was drunk, belligerent, tangled up in a dusty, poorly choreographed fistfight. He stumbled, then, into little Brian, the other kind of boy if there are two kinds of boys. Brian, who was happily carrying a basket brimming with fresh, doomed eggs. They broke all over Main Street. Their yolks, true country yellow.

At the mill, Dr. Mike has the poisoned boy swallow charcoal. It does the trick, drinks up the mercury. And Harding promises to change his ways. And Willow Creek rinses itself clean. And Sully helps Michaela fashion her hair. His hands make you ill with desire. He combs his fingers through her hair but then reaches for her brush—silver and horsehair. And so every ailment has a remedy, every meanness, every wrongness, is forgiven in an hour.

/ ~

Dr. Quinn is exercising. She's swapped her pioneer skirts for black leggings. She's on her back, doing bicycles on the beach.

There's no beach on the frontier. This is not Dr. Quinn but the actress, Jane Seymour, selling you something. She wants you to feel like you really need it but also like it's no big deal.

She says, *Anxiety? Anxiety is believing I'd never get my waist back after having twins. Not getting rid of a few gray hairs.* You have no gray hairs. You are kids. But you do have waists, and waists can be a problem at any age. She studies hers in a full-length mirror, wearing a trim white dress. Her waist is slim, flat, a blank piece of paper. She holds her babies, who are acceptably fat. She has managed to bicycle all of her fat into them.

Waists are obviously a whole thing. But what she's selling is the hair dye, Loving Care. And Jane Seymour cannot stress enough how inconsequential Loving Care is. How filming this commercial is basically a waste of her time and she should probably be getting back to the bicycles. She says, *With Clairol Loving Care, there's no risk. It's got no ammonia, no peroxide, and washes out in 6–12 shampoos.*

Loving Care hardly has any ingredients at all. It barely exists. She says, *Full-time motherhood and a full-time career, now that's a commitment.* You see a fax machine. Fax machine means career. The fax coming through says, *Fax.*

She says, *Loving Care? It's just a little box of hair color.*

Buy it or don't. What difference does it make? You're no leading lady.

/ ~

Ingrid lives in the immigrant camp on the outskirts of town. Matthew, Dr. Mike's oldest, falls hard. At the Hurdy Gurdy, he buys up all of her dance tickets. He proposes. But before they make it to the altar, the girl gets hurt feeding little Brian's sick dog. She gets rabies. *The rabies.* It's quick. And though this is no way to go, she goes.

Poor Ingrid. The episode isn't even about her. It's about the brothers, Matthew and Brian. The dog belongs to Brian. Brian blames himself. The girl belongs to Matthew. His grief is bigger. He is desperate to show how big. By the end, the brothers wrap their arms around each other. Because Ingrid is in a hole. And the dog is baring his wet teeth, crazed, unhuggable. Sully shoots it. He's swapped out his tomahawk. Sometimes this is what care looks like.

You forget Ingrid entirely. You tend to forget. You tend to your forgetting, feed it. You misremember that Colleen, the sister, got rabies. That Colleen was the one grabbing her throat, desperate with hydrophobia. You remember Colleen convulsing in the damp bed, staring at some invisible apparition. But what happens to Colleen is she is recast. The first Colleen is a messy, shaggy-banged blonde. The second Colleen looks like you, an uptight redhead. The two would have never been friends. You are faithful to the first Colleen, refuse to embrace the second Colleen so thoroughly that you scowl when she, too, becomes a doctor. She's doing it wrong.

/ ~

Sometimes there are two snakes around the stick. Sometimes the stick has a set of wings. This symbol is the caduceus. See it in the logos of the American Cancer Society and US Army Medical Corps. But it doesn't mean healing. It doesn't belong to Asclepius. The caduceus belongs to Hermes, god of merchants and thieves and chaperone to the dead journeying to the underworld.

It's been hard to shake that second snake. While the American Medical Association, which used the caduceus for a time, was able to get things sorted out and single-snaked by 1912, the double-snaked version remains ubiquitous in visual culture around medicine. And when the *American Journal of Psychiatry* was called out for using the caduceus in 2011, the editor responded,

> *Asclepius is named in the opening lines of the Hippocratic Oath. As physicians, we must first do no harm and then do our best to learn from our mistakes. Now that the Caduceus has survived more than a century as the erroneous medical symbol, who is to say that it is still a mistake? Perhaps our task, as psychiatrists, is not to correct this error once again, but to study the reasons for its persistence.*

Sometimes the snakes show their tongues, forked. Sometimes the snake is not a snake. Sometimes the staff is not a staff, but a tiny stick, useful in treating *Dracunculus medinensis,* or guinea worm. Which makes the snake a worm, extracted from your body, coiling around the stick, slowly over time.

You don't read about guinea worm when browsing the AMA guide as kids, but you have other favorites: color photographs of eczema worse than yours, illustrations of reproductive organs, and a gallery of close-up images of eyes and open mouths, afflicted with terrible things. Corneal ulcers. Black hairy tongue. You open the book on the floor, kneel over it, stare into everything that might undo you. *You have black hairy tongue. No, you have black hairy tongue. No backsies.*

The true prize is the set of coffee-colored pages in the center of the book. The self-diagnosis charts. You eat them up. You open to whatever page wants to be opened. You see each localized ailment—dizziness, pain in the shoulder, difficulty walking—as equally possible. These charts are paths to follow. Yes. No. The destination can be innocuous, post-nasal drip. But quite often our charts conclude, *Emergency. Seek Medical Attention Now. You might be having a heart attack!* It is thrilling to might be having a heart attack and to close the book and tell no one.

The illustration paired with heart attack is a naked man with a shadow on his chest. Fever is a woman looking down at a mercury thermometer, looking down so much that she might be asleep. Meningitis is a figure covering their tender eyes with their hands. A common cold has a shag haircut and covers her mouth with a white handkerchief. She seems beautiful; you want her to be beautiful. But it all depends on that mouth.

/   ~

On the luckiest day of his life, a man struggles to speak. He's an expert on something. Something historical. American. Something old. Maybe this is a museum or maybe this is just his private, obsessive collection.

He's eating his lunch and listening to the radio, classical, the Vienna Wood Dance in D. But then it's trivia time. They ask the question. He knows the answer. His phone rings, close up on the phone. He is the lucky listener.

The question, *Who shot Alexander Hamilton?* is a question destined for him. The man has an oil painting of the famous duel on display. He has books, relics, the clothes the men wore. He has the gun. He has the very bullet, under a glass dome. It is suspended mid-air somehow, like it might not be done killing.

But when he goes to answer, his mouth is full of sandwich. Peanut butter on soft, cheap bread. He reaches for a carton of milk, finds only drops. *Aaron Burr!* he yells. Unintelligible. He wants credit for knowing. He wants the prize money so he can buy more memorabilia. He wants milk. Oh God, if only he had milk, he would be understood. No one would wonder why he kept what he kept. No one would wonder why he was so obsessed with the past, with these two figures, circling each other, a lump in each of their throats.

/   ~

The medicine show rolls into town with fanfare, a parade. There's a one-man band managing accordion, tambourine, harmonica, and drum. There's an exotified showgirl and, on horseback, a genuine Kickapoo Indian, *Sick-no-more*. Well, Cheyenne sold as Kickapoo but who's counting. For sale is *Dr. Eli's Kickapoo Indian Sagwa*. Also known as *Dr. Eli's Kickapoo Indian Golden Elixir*. Says the bottle, *A compound of the virtues of Roots, Herbs, Barks, Gums, and Leaves. Its elements are Blood-making, Blood-cleansing, and Life-sustaining. It is the Purest, Safest, and Most Effective Cathartic Medicine known to the public.*

Dr. Mike's not biting. Even when it turns out that Doc Eli is an actual doctor, Johns Hopkins by the way. So why this, now? Why a gifted surgeon turned snake oil salesman? She extracts his story until she's tangled up in it. It's a story about the war, Gettysburg, what he saw, what limbs he sawed off. What he heard—soldiers, boys—crying for their mamas. *That's enough*, she says. She says it twice. Leaves him with his elixir. Let it fix the ailments it promises to fix: torpid liver, brain fever, paling cheeks, and wasted manhood. Let him curl up with his bottle of gold. She's off to make an incision.

/   ~

On page 241 there is a photograph of an ear. Behind the ear, a large, fleshy growth. Practically another, baby, ear. It's called a keloid. It's scar tissue run amok. Sometimes the body's capacity to heal itself goes overboard, doesn't know when to stop. Scar tissue keeps growing and growing, healing and healing. Relentless healing. The keloid, you read, can happen in response to the slightest injury, even a piercing. And in fact this keloid photograph is paired with a drawing of a pierced ear. The before image. Hair tucked behind the ear. The earring a small, tasteful hoop. None of you have pierced ears, will ever have pierced ears, and maybe it's because none of you are the pierced ears kind of girl but who's to say it's not because these images—the hoop, the keloid—are etched into your imaginations, forever bound together.

/   ~

Season Three ends with Sully and Dr. Mike's wedding. Season Four ends with a baby. Come Season Six and Michaela is pregnant again. Meanwhile the town is preparing for Founder's Day. Picnic blankets and parasols. A fiddle, a flag. Some are festive but others argue over what is worthy of the time capsule they plan to bury. Grace's recipes. Hank's whiskey. A copy of the *Gazette*. A fishhook. The barber suggests, *Hair clippings from my shop?* to show how absurd it is to make meaning in this way. Are these artifacts or symptoms? The schoolchildren roll out butcher paper, sketch out a chronology of the town, everything they remember and everything they have been told, and the men argue about when the timeline should begin. How much of the past they are willing to preserve.

If the camera panned back to show you, it would show the back of you, sitting on the floor, watching the 19-inch TV tucked into the TV cabinet, a delightfully specific and purposeful piece of furniture. The doors of the cabinet are opened out like wings, the frontier is lit up inside. If the camera panned back further, it would show couches stacked with newspapers. Bookcases stacked with figurines. A buffet blocked by thrift shop chairs and topped with so many dusty framed portraits that most of the faces are hidden. It would show gold curtains, drawn closed over the picture window, which your mother often found disconcerting. It let in too much light, showed abundant, improper amounts of the surrounding landscape.

It made her feel exposed.

While the men argue over Founder's Day, Michaela has a miscarriage. And now the time capsule trunk seems one part treasure chest one part coffin. Michaela can't be her own doctor for this one. She needs someone else to look at all of her parts, to be sure that her body has let go of everything it needs to let go.

/   ~

No one has more natural ingredients.

Jane Seymour again. Her fat babies are now toddlers. Milk is no longer enough for them. They need more. And luckily, Gerber has changed their recipe. Gerber has come a long way. Don't judge Gerber by its imperfect past. They've gotten rid of additives, and *No added sugar or starch now means more bananas in Gerber's bananas.* Jane Seymour loves bananas. She loves them so much that her jars of bananas are surrounded by fresh bananas. Same for the green beans and peaches. But especially bananas. One banana is peeled and sliced, as if she was about to cram it into one of the Gerber jars and ran out of room.

There can only really be one Gerber Baby at a time. The twin on the left is more cooperative, although somewhat dead-eyed, as if he's been lightly chloroformed. Jane Seymour asks, *There's nothing better for my Gerber babies, right, boys?* and the drugged baby nods. And then he nods again as the camera eschews his brother entirely, and zooms in on his vacant face, which is then blurred with and replaced by the iconic 1928 sketch of the cute, alert Gerber baby. The only Gerber baby to stand the test of time.

/   ~

There once was a Cheyenne boy so wise they named him Soars Like Eagle. As he grew older, he grew wiser and wiser, till one day, the great birds themselves adopted him, and swept him up into the sky. This is the story that Sully tells little Brian as they watch an eagle in flight. Brian is not wise. He misidentifies the eagle as a hawk. And Sully is so wrapped up in his story, in watching the eagle, that he fails to notice that Brian is climbing an enormous tree. Brian opens his wings, surrenders to gravity, mistakes falling for flying and hits the earth hard.

In the coma, his head is a vessel, filling with blood, pressure. Dr. Mike is not cut out for this. While her boy worsens, she clutches a medical book, stares at the drawing of an anonymous skull. There is blame in the room. A little verbal duel. She blames Sully, blames the story, cries, *Well I'll thank you to stop filling his head with nonsense like this if there's anything left to fill!* But they are approaching the end of the hour, and the surgeon she tried to recruit from St. Louis is stuck in a flash flood, the telegram just came through. And so they forgive. Dr. Mike is going to have to do this by herself. She knows very little about brains, but also, in this tiny world she knows the most about brains. And when she lines up the tools—razor, scalpel, cranial drill—on the metal tray, her hands are steady.

This is how she doctors you.

Dr. Michaela Quinn turns the drill which pushes the screw into the boy's crown. Her son's crown, shaved down to his tender scalp. The only way you will know if she drills enough or not enough is to see if the child regains consciousness before the end credits. The bit spirals through skin and flesh and bone. The doctor's hands are the mother's hands, are your hands in some future way. And then her hands tell her to stop and so she stops.

THE DISTAFF

*The horses fell asleep in their stalls, the dogs in the courtyard, the
pigeons on the roof, the flies on the walls, and even the fire on the
hearth flickered, stopped moving, and fell asleep.*

> ~*Little Briar Rose*, the Brothers Grimm

For much of the Disney version, Sleeping Beauty sleeps. It's
not a hard way to star in a story. Draped on the bed in a lovely
gown, pink then blue then pink. When she wakes, there is no
morning breath, no quick scrub of the armpits at the pedestal sink.
Not even her crown needs straightening, though one hundred years
have passed. She floats into the prince's arms and they waltz until
the drawing goes still, their embrace suspended in a final storybook
page meant to mimic stained glass.

~

The Grimm Brothers don't need a kiss to wake her. The mere bedside presence of a man is enough to do it. As for Basile, a kiss is only
the start. Briar Rose remains unresponsive when a wandering King
carries her to a better bed and rapes her. Nine months later, twins.
Their new, pink mouths search for milk, find her fingers, pull at the
taste of flax and free the splinter at last. Only then does she wake,
naming them Sun and Moon, to locate herself. She agrees, still

groggy, to love the King. He's already married and his wife demands that Sun and Moon be slaughtered and plated for supper. Her fork is pure silver. She relishes the taste of the children until she learns she's been tricked, served lamb by a soft-hearted kitchen clerk.

~

Elsewhere, our heroine smacks of Snow White, of Gretel. She sleeps in a crystal coffin. She stuffs her pockets with bran to map her path home. Her finger is pricked by a bit of raw flax, by a poisoned needle, by a spindle. In the Perrault tale, the old woman who shares her spinning wheel is not to blame. She knows nothing of the curse, longs only to teach what she knows. *Distaff*, she says, naming the wand that keeps the unspun fibers ready, free from tangles. *Here*, she says, *is how you turn one thing into another*. Briar Rose pumps her foot. The wheel has barely started when her finger catches and she falls to the ground. The old woman, Basile tells us, gathers her skirts and runs away. Is running still, right now as I tell this story.

~

Where are the children? What do they do with a splinter on the tongue? Perhaps they spit it onto the castle floor. But in my experience, when a child summons a parent's accumulated daggers, she bundles them, buries them into her own body for safekeeping.

~

Aesop's Crested Lark is the first creation, pumping her wings in the sky before there is any earth in place beneath her. When her father dies (somehow she has a father), she carries his sour body aloft for a week. Finding no earth in which to store him, and no mother with whom to grieve him, she worries him into her own head, which is how she comes to bear that crest on her brow. It is a burial plot. Aesop doesn't say whether or not, by the lark's time, there is enough world for her to build herself a nest in a grassy hollow. If she rests there, alone or with companions, or if she needs to be carried, too, dooming the next bird to be ever alert, to have the next bird's body changed by grief, while the green earth takes its sweet time coming into shape.

~

My skull doesn't bulge with memory, but I am not a beautiful sleeper. I have enormous eyes, the result of shallow orbits, those depressions of bones framing the sockets. And while big eyes are a coveted feature of many cartoon beauties, they have been the routine subject of ridicule in my actual life. And in sleep, well, shallow orbits render my dreaming, often, open-eyed. Zombie-esque. I learn this at one of my first slumber parties, when Melissa Tabolt screams in the middle of the night, summoning her nightgowned mother out of bed. Because *Marianne looks dead!* Years later, when Melissa and I are in middle school, her mother dies of cancer and is the first dead person I ever face. To look at her body feels like a violence. To feast my big, alive eyes on her sewn, powdered features. To pocket a memory of Jan Tabolt, one casket lid away from permanent darkness, looking like she had, only moments ago, freshened her lipstick and fallen asleep.

~

Perhaps I should do as the phobic Hans Christian Andersen did: sleep beside a handwritten sign, declaring, *I only appear to be dead.* It would be true until it wasn't. And maybe I'd find myself one of those safety coffins from the early cholera days, the ones with the bell inside, meant to alert the churchyard if you'd been buried too soon. In our present pandemic, there is a run on lumber. Too many quarantine patios and coffins under construction. Many of our dead are stored, for a spell, in cardboard. In refrigerated tractor trailers. Stacked on top of one another.

~

Andersen's prone princess has a tower of twenty mattresses on her bed. And twenty featherbeds on top of those. Under it all, a single pea, meant to test her sensitivity and thus her claim of royal blood. In the morning, when asked about her night, she wails. She had a terrible go of it! She is bruised from some hard disturbance. And so, she proves delicate enough to marry, sleepless enough to carry a scepter, to don a heavy crown. As for the pea, it is forgotten. Or kept. Maybe slipped into the apron of a thrifty chambermaid, collecting odds and ends to green up her lamb neck stew.

~

Annoyed at pandemic time, I buy a new wristwatch that will tell me new things. How many steps I cover on a Tuesday. Whether I'm getting the kind of sleep that allows for dreaming. I am. Last night, a dream about a dance audition, no masks. A houseplant in a paper bag. Lateness and a pine forest floor. A compromised torso: from the heart up feels certain, purposeful. My arms are firm and deliberate. Something about tennis. But my lower body—belly, hips, legs—lags a few paces behind, blind to the room it moves through, blind to its purpose. The following night, it's a backyard party and a young liar. Teal oil paintings are pinned in the treetops. There is fun that comes with a cost. My sleep, the app tells me, is splintered among fourteen cycles. Blue blinks, charts. Data drawn, rising and falling.

~

My six-year-old has climbed a thin little oak, not a sapling, exactly, but barely strong enough to bear his forty pounds. I see him from my window where I hold a string of virtual meetings. If he falls, it will matter. If I run outside, I risk missing him, or startling him into a plummet. Instead, I drone on about a registration portal, while I observe his smart body negotiate the possibilities. I recall the moment before he fell off the bed, fell in the creek, wiped out in the wet grass. I remember the moment when he hung from the monkey bars in a costume, when his mask fell and he reached for it, when he lost his grip and hit the earth, breaking the elbow. I remember the break as though I witnessed it, though I was inside chopping vegetables. He walked himself to the house, holding his arm in place under his Batman or maybe Pikachu disguise. At which point I realized I had indeed heard the scream, but had judged it to be part of some faraway game, daydream or memory. This time, I clock, he makes it down to earth without a scratch.

~

At the hem of a dream, there is a child with his hand at his throat. I think it's Cole, my child's schoolmate. One day, he was a healthy first-grader, happily marching in the school's Book Character Parade. He dressed as DogMan, a comic book character whose origin story starts with an explosion, two victims. The doctors tell the injured cop, Officer Knight, *Your head is dying*. They tell the police dog, Greg, *Your body is dying*. The only option is to stitch the two living parts together. So one day Cole is DogMan and then another day he catches some virus, which closes his throat while he lies in his bed, while his sister and parents dream.

A year later, I take my boys to see *DogMan* author Dav Pilkey and there is a red cape for every child in the audience. That night, my Nolan wakes with the worst croup they've ever seen at the Children's Hospital. He turns blue on the kitchen floor. But his head doesn't die. His body doesn't die. For weeks he plays that his stuffed animals are suffocating, drowning. They can barely keep their eyes open.

Or the boy in the dream could be Corey, the boy who sat in front of me in seventh grade. Corey used to rock back in his seat, so cool. I held mild concern every time he did it, worried that he would tumble backwards, whack his head on my desk or the classroom floor.

But that's not how Corey died. As I heard it, the summer before he was to start the eighth grade, he played on the beach. Some other little kid was fooling around with a wiffle ball bat and whacked

Corey clean in the throat. His trachea collapsed. Then the rest of him. His mother, I am sure, collapsed beside him. Someone ran to find a telephone, someone whisked the toddler away, someone kicked at the sand, helpless, and someone counted the seconds. Someone listened for breath but could hear only the ocean, which gave them false hope. No one counted the waves, swelling, cresting, breaking, falling, disappearing.

~

Where is David? We are wondering about our brother. It is winter and we have grown tired of sledding, dodging the trees on our hillside. Our wet socks are tucked into the radiator. Our hot drinks steam into our pink faces. David is out there, asleep in the snow, under the maple, concussed. How long until we find him.

~

Where is Emily? Our baby sister has once again wandered down to the neighbor's. Once, she sits in a drainage ditch and returns with an earthworm in her diaper. Once, she climbs up on their porch swing and takes the kind of nap we can never get her to take at home. The neighbors call and we collect her. When she is older, and many of our other siblings have already left us, she threatens to run away when I am babysitting. I help her pack a bag and watch from the picture window overlooking the hillside. Emily makes it surprisingly far, almost out of sight, before she runs back to me, crying. I feel smart and selfish, like a parent in a sitcom.

~

Rip Van Winkle drifts off on purpose. Into the Catskills north of my hometown. No curse, his long sleep is what he's been looking for, some goddamn peace and quiet, away from his nagging wife and needy children. Away from the necessary work of the world. What he sleeps through: the death of his wife, the growth of his children, the graying of his beard, the Revolutionary War, his musket rotting in his own hands, an election.

~

Wake me up in 2020, is what some of us have been inclined to say from time to time, under the toxic leadership of 45. Oh, to drape ourselves on the furniture and be roused at a better time. Of course, we are foolish to think that one villain contains the danger. There are other poisoned spindles. And when 2020 comes, it brings a new nightmare, and then another and another. And many are so bone tired that they wonder how they will summon another breath, while some nights I am ashamed of the size of my dreams. My children, unmasked, embracing their friends. My healthy body, perched on some staircase, curling into itself to protect its own tiny heart. When a mild earthquake wakes my son one morning, he walks into the living room with a sleepy smile. *That was terrifying*, he says. *I thought that was a ghost!* And we are a family laughing together in plaid flannel pants. Laughing about ghosts and fault lines. Online, I read that we are nowhere near a fault line, which is one reason that we haven't felt a quake like this before. It's been more than 100 years, in fact. The news site asks me to click on a government link, a *Did You Feel It?* button.

~

Where I live, the elementary schools like to celebrate the 100th day of school each spring. Kids assemble 100 Legos into useless structures. Late at night, tired teachers cut out 100 strips of construction paper for some sad craft. My son, some Monday, is asked to draw a picture of himself at 100 years old. The idea is that kids will dream big. They'll list their many adult accomplishments. Awards earned, inventions that changed the world, scads of grandchildren, trophies, famous people things. Nolan draws himself lying on the ground with a cane, with tiny Xs for eyes. He writes, *When I am 100, I will be close to dead.*

Another year, his teacher uses some cheap age-progression app to wrinkle him, deaden and uncolor his hair, loosen his sweet freckled kindergarten cheeks into jowls. He is horrified at the result. It brings him to tears. He brings it home. Buries it in the trash.

~

We visit Western New York in the summer and hole up in a little lakefront cottage to comply with the mandatory quarantine before visiting family. In the half-sleep of early morning, I hear the wind and lake at work. I dream that the kayaks are left too close to the shore, that they go missing. I see myself leaping out of bed to save them, and then I fall, hard. When I finally stumble out to the water, the boats are still there, pulsing with the colorless waves. I pull them up on the rocks before my arms are quite awake. I find we are short one oar.

~

Sleep in the Bible is busy with prophecy, but only one woman gets to dream. The unnamed wife of Pontius Pilate, on the eve of Christ's sentencing, tells her husband, *Have thou nothing to do with that righteous man; for I have suffered many things this day in a dream because of him.* There is disagreement about whether the vision came from Heaven or Hell, about the potential, spiraling spiritual implications of rescuing Jesus from his cross.

~

Here, my father said that spring, handing me a book. *For your social studies paper. Salem Witchcraft*, by Charles Wentworth Upham, an ancestor. Published in 1867, often cited as the authoritative text documenting the Salem Witch Trials of 1692. I read it, though much of it is over my head. I have no sense of historical scale, thinking that Upham had witnessed the trials as they happened. In Salem, nineteen of the twenty witches were hanged on Gallows

Hill. The last, Giles Cory, was covered with stones, one at a time, until he was pressed, like a flower, to death. I read about Cotton Mather, his father, Increase. I read about Tituba, who had it up to here with these white girls and their sorry poppets. But it is these girls, these witches, who bewitch me, their lies and sanctity. I love their hysteria, performance, the hallucinations prompted by a fungus in the fields, or a bird-borne sleeping sickness, or girlhood in a world where women were ghosts. Bound to turn on one another, they turned. Every dream was an affliction. Every dream was evidence.

~

Silas, underwater, just out of reach.

~

When we buy our house, the home inspector aims his flashlight at old basement wiring, housed in some deteriorating fiber casing. *Asbestos*, he warns. *You're going to want to seal that up.* We do, but that doesn't stop the dreams from my childhood resurfacing. When my elementary school was shuttered for a year because of asbestos, I dreamed of poison. In the dream, I can't wake anybody up. They are not dead, but they will always be asleep. And the poison gives us animal bodies. Athletic kangaroo legs. Twitching faces and soft long ears. For years in my childhood, I am terrified to be awake alone, terrified to look in the mirror after dark, when the new features are bound to surface. Now when it comes, I know that I am dreaming and there is no terror. But I still try to wake up my sisters. I still walk on unfamiliar legs down the hall in search of my mother.

~

One son falls asleep in seconds. The other can never settle and grows desperate when he finds that I am going to bed. I tell him about Grandma, how she is more of a night owl than the two of us, how when I was a kid I would hear her watching television and shuffling around in her slippers until 2 or 3 in the morning, and it comforted me. *You were lucky*, he says. I was. So for him, I play music while I fold laundry at midnight. I take a long shower, take my time with the hair dryer. I read in bed longer than I need to, or want to, knowing that he will be at the door soon, peeking inside to be sure he is not alone in the waking world.

~

What woke us one night might have been the chandelier crashing to the floor. Or the limb of an unlucky oak, through my child's window. Maybe a fist through a pane in the basement. Or all of our plates abandoning the cupboards all at once. All of our wine bottles, fallen like dominoes, like girls in the aquamusicals with their magic sideways dives and their silver crowns, glittering in the splash. When they rose out of the swimming pool, their crowns were on fire.

~

Nolan, a newborn in the blankets somewhere. The bedding is endless, still sour from the night I labored at home. His hunger is endless. The bedroom walls are empty. Which way is up, out? I lose a day checking every lump in the bed and when I find him he startles, cries out.

~

There's a divot in the wall and it might be from a bullet. Years ago, the former owner of this house walked in the front door with a borrowed gun and shot his wife in the head. My husband and I learn this story shortly after moving in, and then find a shallow depression in the wall. We gauge where the wife might have been seated. Where the husband would have stood, aimed. It seems to add up.

The wife, somehow, survives to this day. Before the pandemic, she would visit our neighbors for tea. Her husband, who was unwell, is no longer alive. I assume he is haunting someone else's house, because he has never surfaced in my dreams.

~

My father's final weeks are marked by somnolence. He'll wake to a kiss, or a firm knock on the door. He'll crack a joke or stare at me like I am a stranger. I bring him coffee. After a lifetime of Folgers, he now prefers a pumpkin spice latte, which I pick up on the way to the nursing home, dumping half of it in the bushes to make it light enough for him to lift. *You're so trendy, Dad*, I say. *You know me*—he starts, as if he'll go on to say *always on the cutting edge* or *I just can't live without my Starbucks*. But he doesn't finish the thought, just stops at *You know me* and falls asleep in his wheelchair.

Another day, he announces, with authority, *Francis Bacon!* Then back to sleep.

When he wakes, he finds me trying on his radiation mask—a horror-worthy white plastic contraption, made for only him and marked with a sharpie where the tumor resides. I don't know why I put it on, don't know what I thought I'd see looking through my dad's gaping sockets. He stares at me with curiosity and maybe disgust. Wearing his mask as if it were a costume. I remove it, set it back on the shelf, his cancer trophy, his proof that he did all he could to survive. He drifts off.

~

Silas, silent, holds my hand as we walk home in the dark. We round Miller Park. A woman gets in my face. She is more than me. She is heavier, older, curly-haired, high-energy. She might be me, might be crazy, dangerous. She wants to teach me something but I'm no fool. I tell her *no*. Silas holds my hand, expressionless, as neutral as a prince. She wanders off. As we come up Rosewood from the park, we spot her out on the ballfield under the moon. She is running, then spinning, joyfully. She looks up at the moon as if she is its mother. Silas and I cross the street to get more distance. We climb the hill. Make it home. Wake me up.

THE THING
THAT   THE
BOY

He fell back, into the snow.
~I Survived the Children's Blizzard by Lauren Tarshis

M y sons say they are going to play in the woods. They are generous—the boys for calling them woods. But also the woods—just a meager patch of trees—for growing whatever little wonders and dangers they can manage, hemmed in as they are by streets, houses, us. This is no middle of nowhere. This is the middle of where. Where the moss   . Where the kudzu and the   ivy climb. Where it is impossible to be lost. Where no one will ever dig out a home. The land is too steep, cut through with a creek that never rushes, and never dries up.

To the west, the Murder House. We were new to the neighborhood when I heard a megaphone at 3 a.m. I thought I was dreaming. The woman on the megaphone had a lot of things to say. I could not make out a single word and so I thought she must be saying them to me. I thought, maybe, I was losing my mind. This, after so many of years of worrying I would lose my mind followed by a slow relief as I aged past the most likely window for mind-losing. It turned out the woman, who was real, was a SWAT team. Not the whole team. Just the team's voice, calling into the house where a mother lived with her adult son. Where her adult son was hiding from a man he owed something. Where that owed man came and shot the mother, who some said was to blame for living with her adult son. The way they said *adult*. How she should have had limits. How the shot mother, dead mother, should have had   . Given how her son was, given the company he kept, given the things he got up to.

Never Eat Shredded Wheat is a device for remembering the four cardinal directions. My brother was in a cover band called Shredded Wheat. Their one music video begins with four pieces of the cereal lined up against a blank white wall. In the next shot, the cereal has been replaced by four teenaged boys. They sit on the floor. They are nowhere. They don't know where to put their legs, so they send them straight out. The camera is low, privileging the bottoms of their dirty sneakers, all they've stepped on. The soles outsize their young faces, which are blemished but free of shadow.

To the south, the green house of the woman who lost her dog, walked the neighborhood frantically calling his name. *Peaches.* The dog called back but she didn't hear him. I say *him* because I am one of those people who think of dogs as boys and cats as girls for no good reason. She didn't hear Peaches because she was wearing headphones. She must be one of those people who need a soundtrack, who need to feel like they are in a movie in order to feel like they are not in a movie.

A compass is another device. Put Red Fred in the Shed is a device for properly using that device. No one says what makes Fred red. No one says if the red is blood or if it's Fred's or if a device is to blame. No one says what will happen to Fred once he goes inside.

To the east, the big house, with the five kids. With the toddler who wandered into my front yard alone, having crossed Magnolia, where people drive like bats out of hell, which is to say, fast. Which is to say that the bats aren't there of their own accord. The boy's eyes were full of wonder. I took his hand to walk him home. *I know you,* I said to him, though it wasn't true. I only knew where to put him. The father appeared then,   with worry, in a car. I gave him the child, nearly certain, how certain can you be, that this boy belonged to this man.

My friend   says it at a potluck. *When my son was kidnapped.* The kidnapping isn't the story; it's only framing, only bones for some other story. *When my son was kidnapped.* But some of us have never heard of this kidnapping. It happened years ago, before we ever met. The boy was little, stolen by the ex. The boy was impossible to find for two years. He was gone. Then he was back. But it was so long ago. So many other remarkable things have happened since that remarkable thing. We want to know everything, to assuage our guilt for knowing nothing. What else have we

          ? Which one of us   the   ? And maybe we just failed to ask the right questions.

Magnolia cuts north/south. When we moved here, the road had no sidewalks but the autumn my oldest started preschool up the street, sidewalks appeared. It was as if the sidewalk was built only for me, as if the city poured the cement and the cement hardened before me as I walked, unrushed, pushing the stroller to Temple Emmanuel. At 8:45, I'd walk to Temple, pushing him in the stroller. At 9:05 I'd push the empty stroller home, as there was no obvious place to leave the stroller and it also felt like an experiment. Me, a mother. Me, not a mother.

My mother loses vision in one eye. There is a pain in her head and half of her field of vision goes dark. Half of her field. She tells no one for a week. She waits to see what happens.

What happens is no one asks, *Janet, can you see out of both of your eyes?*

No one asks, *Does one eye feel like a widow, Janet?*

Eventually she volunteers the information and doctors say she will be okay. It's just a narrowing vessel, a hardening. She only needs a needle pushed into her eye once a month for three months.

She only needs   . Which of her seven children is going to take her. Some of us have a thing about eyes and we quietly gag or mime gagging. Gagging is the throat pushing away the unswallowable.

My mother never
         the   .
WTF. Just. Wow. my siblings text. Wow, the shadow of Mom.

To the north, my house. The mossy, uneven yard. The rotting sandbox where the boys used to bury and dig, bury and dig. The untended garden beds. The soccer net, rope line, its easy obstacles. The neighbors. Betty, Sarah, Bruce, Gene, Beth, Beth, Mark, Steve, Max, Lauren,   . The man who yells at   . The man who smashes a guitar in the street in broad daylight. The man who is sick and now the sirens come for different reasons and there is a new, troubling gentleness. He and   take a slow walk. We search his face, trying to gauge his pain. *He looks good*, we say. Or *He doesn't look good.*

Before the house was ours, the house belonged to a doctor, who failed to care for it. He left behind a basement full of rubbish. He left behind takeout containers and roaches. He left, in a drawer, a commemorative coin from some bachelor party, some boy ritual. It's engraved with the words *Dave and Mick Lick Tit*. Engraved. Before the doctor, Hazel. One night Hazel's husband borrowed a gun from a neighbor. Hazel's husband borrowed the gun for some seemingly legitimate reason, then walked into his house, our house, where

Hazel sat in an armchair, where I curl up on the couch. Maybe she was reading a mystery. Maybe knitting. Did she knit. Was she folding fresh warm linens. Am I folding. Anyway the thing I've been saving up to say is he shot her in the head.

Here's a groove in the wall. I want to know if it's Hazel's. I want my husband and me to find the exact angle, I want him to   the screen door, that would have had to be part of it. I want to try out different   . I want to feel a startle, to say *Hello* and then *What on earth are you doing with a gun?* I want my husband to turn his hand into the universal sign for a gun and I want him to shoot our wall to bits so we will never have to think, exactly, about what happened to Hazel. If everything is ruined then no one is a target. I want to forget Hazel with a hole in her, even as I remember that Hazel survived being shot in the head. That she still comes around the neighbor's place. Bruce and Sarah's. We always say their names in that order. Bruce and Sarah give her tea. Bruce and Sarah offer sugar, honey, milk.

Here are the titles.

I Survived the Japanese Tsunami

I Survived the Battle of Gettysburg

I Survived the Shark Attacks of 1916

I Survived the   of Pompeii

I   the Battle of D-Day

I Survived Hurricane Katrina

I   the Sinking of

I Survived the Children's Blizzard

I have never heard of the Children's Blizzard. My son, obsessed with these stories of fake children facing real horrors, teaches me. It's winter in North Dakota, 1888. A sunny morning. Then, wind. Snow falls. The temperature falls. Children, trying to get home from school, lose footing, fall into snowbanks. Become indistinguishable from snowbanks. Become snow. 213 children die in that weather.

The accumulation totals less than two inches, but the texture of the snow is *like flour, filling the lungs*. The children disappear on their way to their homes, their mothers, to the fragrant lunches the mothers have prepared. Hot soup. Fresh brown bread. Golden butter. Or marmalade if you like, whatever you like.

In September, a 15-year-old shoots and kills another 15-year-old at a nearby high school. District lockdown. Text alerts. The shooter is on the run, on foot. My sister lives in the neighborhood and gets a message from law enforcement.

Stay in your house. Stay away from your windows.

The shooter is cutting through backyards. Does he notice the swing sets. Did he used to have one like those when he was small. When did he stop being small.

Because of the police, I have to drive a new way to pick up my own children from their school downtown. My third grader's classroom is windowless and hard to find. He likes that. It's right next to the utility closet, where they practice   . Where the kids who wear light-up shoes are chastised for tempting Fate.

The victim's name is William Miller, the first and last name almost-mirrors. William the word at the edge of a stagnant body of water. Miller the reflection. I'm holding back. Because he's William Miller Junior. Which changes the reflection. Which means presumably there is a different, maybe alive, William Miller. And so maybe it was this other William Miller's mother who liked *l*'s and near-symmetry like I like *l*'s and near-symmetry. My boys are Nolan. Silas. At one time, Silas has some stuffies he's named Silas Junior and Silas Junior Junior. He thinks this is how Juniors work. Nolan and Silas are not themselves Juniors, although occasionally older gentlemen in grocery stores will refer to them as such.

Junior.

Or *Son.*

Or *Young Man.*

It's not long until the killer is named in the papers. Turns out he is also a Junior.

William Miller Junior's mother. I mean, William Chavis Renard Miller Junior's mother. She says her boy was

joyful, amazing.

She says that on the day of the shooting, he woke up late for school. She told him not to go, to stay home. He wanted

.   She says,

He was going down the hall. I saw the side of his face.

I promise Silas I will stay with him until he falls asleep. His mind is in chaos with all of these stories. *These things really happened, Mom.* He tells me that during the Children's Blizzard, a teacher fastened a long rope around her waist, bound herself to a line of a dozen children. Her house was not far and, by some blinding, uneven grace, they arrived there.

We are both thinking it. *Do we have enough rope here. Do we have any.*

We murmur our little murmurs. We warm under a shared blanket. When he is almost asleep, I can smell it. Some chemical shift in the composition of his breath. I don't know if everyone has this. I have only lain so close to precious few bodies on the brink. It smells like the opposite of snow. It smells like a thaw, alive. It's heady, I lean in for it. It is good. It is not good. His brother has it, too, his own personal variation. Maybe I have mine. But this boy here, his scent is inherited. It's a wonder. He smells exactly like his father, falling over the edge.

There is a gun in the cellar of my childhood, hanging on the wall. I don't know about guns, their varieties. Its barrel is long. Does that help. Does that make it a rifle. A shotgun. My mother gets it from her brother, who she trusts knows his way around the objects of men. She wants the gun for bears. Bees. Coyotes. She would be better in a city. In tap shoes and taxi cabs. She would. She never wanted   woods.

The cellar is enormous, a perfect shadow of our hilltop ranch home. Other families would have painted, carpeted, ping-pong tabled it. Other families would have had it *finished*. Would have bragged that it was *finished*. Instead, we keep it gray, fill it with the gun and with broken things we do not have the heart to toss. We come down here for the laundry, only. The laundry which we run two, three times through, until there is no scent of soap left. We dodge mouse droppings and a shattered jar of pennies at the foot of the stairs. Nobody is allowed to sweep them up because sweeping them up will send the wrong things into the air. Shards of glass. Viruses. Waiting to enter our lungs.

I am coming up the cellar stairs, a basket of bedding hooked on my bony hip. My mother stands above, at the top. She could push me down these stairs right now. She could. It would be easy. I would land in the pennies, glass, droppings. In the fall, a blank pillowcase, worn so thin, would catch the air, much like the sheer scarves we used to toss in ballet class. They had so little mass. We could throw them with all of our might and they would barely go anywhere.

My father wanted no part of the gun in the cellar and because of this I thought he must be gentle.   I thought
        . When he has a sudden, anaphylactic reaction to aspirin, my mother saves his life. Because she has several deadly allergies of her own (shellfish, almonds, guinea pigs, dashing her hopes of becoming a biomedical researcher), she keeps an epi pen, which she plunges into my father's thigh with the calm of a nurse, which she is. He has never been allergic to aspirin before but that's how it can go. Sometimes the body finds it has a limit. Sometimes the body has a reaction.

I have heard, of violence and of valor, *I didn't know they had it in them*. I mean, didn't you?

Sleep-starved, I nurse my newborn. Finally, finally, he begins to drift off. His brother, two, is having none of it. None sleep. None books. None me holding the baby. He pushes open the door, runs at us, a *No* in his throat. I hold out my one available hand, like a crossing guard. I whisper, *Stop!* All he hears is my voice is soft. All he sees is a hand that might hold him. He runs into it, and it fails to yield. I fail to yield. He falls to the floor, wails, *You pushed me!* And maybe I did. And now the baby is awake. And now the baby is awake forever.

Half of the field is real grass. Half of the field is turf. Dozens of kids, mostly boys, run drills, don pinnies, chug Gatorade. I'm one of the moms who walks the perimeter, watching the sunset, listening to a podcast. We always circle in the same direction, with an air of self-satisfaction. Not because we are exercising, but because our children are. There is nothing better, we think, than these kids running around, than seeing their breath make shapes in the cold air. It feels like, with our circling, our boring a groove in the earth and the fake earth, we are keeping them here, keeping them safe.

On one edge, the nets back up against chain link. We time our movements, then, scoot quickly behind these nets. Tonight, a teenager kicks the ball into the hole of the goal just as I step behind it. I wince. Nothing more. I just do what a body does when a projectile   , when a body doesn't trust a net. The boy apologizes profusely. *You're fine,* I say. *This is your field,* is what I mean.

My son's coach speaks Spanish and so his coaching is full of unfamiliar words. Some are nicknames for the kids. Some are terms I can't discern, despite several years of high school Spanish, despite doing just fine in Bolivia. I ask Silas what his coach is yelling. He tells me some things. *It means we need to call it, to use our voices.* Or *it means pass it backwards.* But mostly, *You don't have to know all the words, Mom.*

The thing about a gun is the hole in it.

The thing about a hole is that the inside of the hole is called a barrel or a bore but it is not boring.

The thing about boring is if the story goes where you expect the story to go and if that path is well-worn, bored through.

If a gun doesn't fire in Act I it must fire in Act II, but if lots of other guns fire then maybe it doesn't have to. Maybe firing would be boring. Maybe the gun can just perch on the wall. Chekhov says if a gun is on the wall then the wall is the one holding the gun. Chekhov says if shots ring out in the neighborhood then casings are littered in the yard and your neighbor will find them when she is hanging laundry on the line. Chekhov says if your toddler finds a used drug needle at a Montessori playground you have to keep testing your toddler for hepatitis and HIV because it can take a while for the tests to show what's multiplying in his bloodstream. Chekhov says not to Google *how long does HIV live on a Goldfish cracker.* Or *what if you just poke it a little to see if it is sharp can you get HIV.* Chekhov says if you fill a gun with cut flowers the flowers could still be poisonous. They could be larkspur, lily of the valley, foxglove, leather flower. Chekhov says if a barrel of a gun is tied into a knot, the hole is still a hole. Even if it can't be untied. Even if the artist, Carl Fredrik Reuterswärd, has been dead for eight years. No bullets there. Just pneumonia. Chekhov says we are usually concerned with guns when we should be concerned with lungs. Chekhov says we are usually guns when we should be lungs. Chekhov dies of tuberculosis. My father dies of a brain tumor, which longs to be a hole and in that way is a hole. My father has respiratory problems as a child. Chekhov says if your lungs are guns you cannot breathe. You can only hang on the wall, waiting to be held.

We have a man to kill. His name is Pierre. My son has been saving up for Pierre and now he is here, with the spring. Pierre is six feet tall and my husbands' clothes fit him eerily well. We have to pin the waist of his jeans to the hem of his long-sleeve t-shirt because every time he dies, his top rides up, revealing his cheap cotton body, the polyfill already emerging through the seams. When Pierre was sewn, he was probably sewn inside out, an empty sack. That's how sewing something like this works. At some point, the man or woman or child with the needle pulled his entire skin through an unsewn hole. Then somebody else, probably, stuffed him. Then somebody else, probably, sewed up the hole.

Pierre, I don't know why he is French, is like a newborn. No head control. The only thing about him that does not flop is his hands. They are rubber, oversized, graying, like they already know what they will do.

I'm not buying any new Halloween decorations this year, I announce. I am always trying to get things to count for other things.

We will use Pierre to scare the trick-or-treaters. But until then, Pierre is a stuntman for home movies. My son, half Pierre's size, coordinates his wardrobe with Pierre's. Sets up his iPad. Shoots footage of himself climbing the magnolia. Shoots Pierre falling from the magnolia. Shoots himself running towards the cliff above the creek. Shoots Pierre, thrown, crashing into the creek, limbs every which way. Pierre loses his cap, my son's cap, in the fall. It's a newsboy cap, which my boy has been wearing since watching the 1968 musical *Oliver!* And he shares the cap with Pierre. *Pierre!*

At night, it becomes my job to bring Pierre into the basement, where I curl him up into himself, back into the shape he took when he arrived in a wet cardboard box. I drape one of our lesser blankets over him. I am tucking him in for the night. I am hiding him because no one in this family wants to be surprised, especially in the morning. Especially in the afternoon. Especially in the middle of the night, when any number of reasons might send us from our beds.

I wanted to see where you were.

I had a dream I didn't know was a dream.

Are you   ?

Do you need   ?

What do you need?

What can I do?

What happened to your ?

I heard something.

It was too quiet.

It sounded like .

IF YOU GATHERED

*In the past 24 hours, did you have close contact with anyone who
has tested positive for Covid-19?*
~Daily Wellness Survey, Wake Forest University,
March 2020–May 2021

Overall, do you consider yourself healthy?

We have gotten away.

My girlfriends and I have pressed pause on our jobs, kids, kitchens, for a winter retreat near Fancy Gap. Girls trip. Self-care. Jess and Leah have gone to bed, but I stay up by the woodstove fire to stare, to bask, to see how far my mind will wander. I take no credit for the fire. I am not a fire starter. And, it turns out, I am also not a fire stopper. Because when I am ready to rest, I find I can't stop the burn. I close the flue, I think, but the fire hums along. Google offers no consensus on whether or not it is safe to fall asleep while flames pulse in the center of your house. I close the flue and wait longer but the fire doesn't care. I open the flue, try to speed up the burn, to no avail. So I doze, upright on the couch, let my dropped head tug me awake every few minutes, until the fire quiets of its own accord.

I don't tell my friends because I'm embarrassed, and also distracted. In between Googling *Can I go to sleep if a fire is burning?* and learning about creosote, I've been reading about Wuhan. A virus. I don't say much about this either. We are supposed to be away. So we write, feast, rest, and talk with perfect rhythm. As we come and go from the cabin for easy little adventures, we notice the neighboring lot, a farm, where thin horses trudge through mud, hooves unclipped. We see goats standing in the rain. What is our role? Neighbor, sort-of. Outsider. No knowledge of this family. No sense of the fate of these animals if we call the county anyway. We turn away, together.

Before we pack up to leave the mountains behind, Leah takes our photo. The sky is clear. We hold one another close and beam smiles towards our future selves. This is already becoming a memory. Jess wears a sweatshirt printed in eyes, some open, lucky lashed, others closed. When I arrive home, I find my children lounging on beach towels in the backyard, shirtless and squinting in the sunshine. Even in Carolina, 70 is a little wild for January, a little off.

In the past 24 hours, did you gather with one or more persons outside your immediate household?

My husband and I squeeze our bodies into folding chairs at *The Grey Eagle* to see an old favorite of mine from college days, singer-songwriter Dar Williams. The last time I saw her would have been at Floydfest more than a decade ago. I've lost track of her recent albums, but it doesn't matter. She is exactly the same. *As Cool as I Am* reminds me of college girlfriends, a wild and lovely slumber party at Rachel's upstairs apartment on Main. We declared the night *The Glitter Symposium*. We dressed like goddesses. We cooked, sang, danced, ate, circled up on the floor and made pillows of one another's laps, embracing Dar's anthem, *I will not be afraid of women.* Outside, some of the men in our orbit called up from the street, asking to be let inside. We refused. One wrote on the sidewalk, with a bottle of ketchup he carried for some reason, maybe this reason, *Glitter Is Apartheid!*, which he thought we would find charming. Which, good Lord, we did. Although we still did not let them in.

Dar's voice hasn't aged. *You're just two umbrellas*, she reminds us. It's depressing, her sameness. *What do you love more than love?* On the stage, she bumps elbows with a bass player, a half-joke about contagion. It's March. Things will shut down in two weeks. This will be my last crowd for more than a year but I don't know to savor it. I remember we had some dumb argument. I remember we parked far from the club and the ground was a sheet of ice. We clung to one another, trying not to slip. We were laughing, lit by love, going towards the music. I remember there was an opener.

If you gathered, did you wear a mask?

I have enough panic and money that I sign up for grocery delivery. I ask for disinfecting wipes and avocados, organic milk and Doritos. I ask that the bags be left on our stoop, where I will wash down every item with the disinfecting wipes should they be in stock. Produce is tough. A doctor on YouTube says I should tumble my oranges and cucumbers into a clean, soapy sink. But my sink is never clean and can one wash bananas? When the Instacart driver pulls up to the curb, I watch through the front window. From behind her mask, she appears to be about my age with a droopy blonde ponytail bound with a scrunchy. She wears a leg brace, and it is with obvious discomfort that she steps up on the sidewalk from the street, opens her van's sliding door. She carries the first few bags—all plastic, and therefore holding just a few items each—up the walkway, leaves them on my stoop. Then, a calculated, lopsided pivot to return to the van to do it again. I'm embarrassed of my own decadence. I peel a mask from a doorknob and step outside. *Can I help you?* I ask her, a question that, depending how you ask it, sometimes means *Can I help you?* but sometimes means, *Just what do you think you are doing here?* I mean it the first way. *Are you comfortable if I stay distant?* She is more than happy to allow me to unload my own damn groceries. She moves to stand under our blooming dogwood tree, commanding the space framed by the pink canopy as if there is an X under her feet. Her tree.

Her van is littered with cereal, wrappers, and dirt, and shares with my car the distinct kid odor I call *hot snacks*. There are so many bags, and they have slid deeper into her van in transit. I'm halfway inside, breathing her family's air, contaminating her family's air with my family's air. Later in the pandemic, it will be second nature to hold or shallow my breath, but I'm not there yet. On my final trip, I pull out a case of lime La Croix, a bougie habit we will abandon by summer, simply because we tire of carrying it. Our driver drives away and I take stock of our front stoop. The colorless bags are too small for the FAMILY SIZE box of Cheerios, are doubled up for the single cantaloupe. The handles remain upright, alert. They look like garden shoots, alive and organized.

If you gathered, did you wash your hands or use hand sanitizer?

The first text I receive each morning comes at 7:04. *Don't forget to take your Daily Wellness Survey!* And I do not forget. Just like I do not forget to go for a run, to count my steps, to send my boys outside at the same time each day for what I now call *recess*. I do not forget to let my mail sit untouched for 48 hours, to water my plants, to walk my boys through the neighborhood when I hear that multiple neighbors have posed teddy bears in their front windows so that kids can have something cute to hunt. We find them, count them. On Westfield, one bear is mashed between blinds and glass, and stays there for many months. A sweet gesture seemingly forgotten, a person who never otherwise bothers with those blinds. At first I think the teddy bear hunt is a neighborhood thing, but then I learn there is a viral global trend. Some say it is inspired by the children's book, *We're Going on a Bear Hunt* by Michael Rosen. When the trend peaks, Rosen is unavailable for interviews because he is sick with Covid. He ends up hospitalized, on a vent for six weeks. Before he is admitted, he posts his pain on Twitter: *Every other muscle from toes to scalp shouting, And me. And me. And me. And me.*

If you gathered, did you undergo Covid-19 testing prior to gathering? Are you experiencing? Did you wear?

My sister is in labor so I drive through a thunderstorm to stay with her older daughter while she and her husband head to the hospital. It's about five in the morning and luckily the child doesn't wake. I rest in the guest bed, listening to the rain, wearing a mask made from kitchen curtains I grew tired of, a pattern of bird shadows and orange teardrops. I plan to wear a mask for the next two days. But when Libby wakes up a couple of hours later, I have taken it off in my sleep, kept it in my fist while I dreamed. I'm reminded of my various failed attempts to sleep with a mouth guard at night. I'm a jaw-clencher, especially in times of stress, especially now. They say that the pressure of clenching your jaw at night is the equivalent to having a linebacker stand on your mandible. When I picture him, he can only fit one cleat in my mouth. But his balance is perfect. He is calm and steady. And he is not cruel about it; he's just heavy. So far, he's broken two of my molars. But every time I try to sleep with a pricey mouth guard, it ends up lost in the sheets or flung across the room. Only the muddy cleat will do.

In the backyard, Libby keeps asking me to play with her, to which I respond, *This is me playing.* I'm keeping us outdoors as much as possible, to lower transmission risk. And I'm keeping my distance. She settles for this as the game. *Six feet!* She sings, *Nuh-uh-uh!* when she sneaks up close. I stretch out on the bright yellow slide, stare into the sky. She swings. We name things we like. Yellow. Purple. Puddles. Babies. By the evening, she needs proximity. The last time her mother went to the hospital to have a baby, the baby went straight to Heaven. So we snuggle on the couch. I wear a mask and read her stories. I wonder if it is strange for her to have an aunt who looks and sounds so much like her own mother. When I swap my contacts for my glasses, pull my hair into a ponytail and pull my sister's afghan over my lap, does the comfort of my almost-Emilyness inoculate her daughter from the twin feeling of disquiet? Or maybe my scent, my posture, my storytelling cadence is so distant from my sister's that it doesn't cross Libby's mind at all. Maybe her nearness is not my nearness. Not even close.

What symptoms are you experiencing? What symptoms are yourself?

Curbside pickup day at the elementary school. My kids haven't been here in weeks, haven't been downtown at all. I drive the wrong way in the car loop, already forgetting the weekday traffic pattern. Masked teachers hand us packets through the window. The teachers, with their sturdy, loving, layered voices, they always make me cry, and I cry. After, we park and go for a walk, taking Trade Street, past the bus station. Up ahead, a small crowd of folks hanging around, waiting for a ride. None of them are masked. A few smoke cigarettes, making the trajectory of their breath visible, cartoonish. I want to change course but I fret about how my kids will see my reaction, what they will learn from my decision to go a different way when faced with a group of mostly Black people simply existing, mostly Black people who might be just as quickly deemed scary if they were wearing masks. The group seems far enough from the sidewalk. But then, as we approach, an older man walks within a couple of feet and coughs, productively and repeatedly, into the air we breathe. Soon, after, I decide that I will cross every street, dodge everybody forever.

Among the school materials we've picked up are two novels, *Holes* and *My Side of the Mountain.* Books about monotony, containment, liberation. I wonder if these were the planned books, or if the teacher has chosen them to satisfy fourth grade pandemic imagination. The game Candyland, I once read, was invented by a teacher being treated in a children's polio ward in the '40s. What those kids longed for, as they languished in drab iron lungs arranged in a rigid grid, was color, curves, movement, and luck. Because luck is the only way to win. You can't be good at Candyland. You can't practice and get any better.

Overall, do you consider yourself?

The sewing starts in the spring, a friend calling for help making masks for local healthcare facilities, which are dangerously low on PPE. PPE, one of the new words I find on my tongue. It tastes like licorice. Lose a turn. It tastes like the walls of our peanut brittle houses.

The masks are easy. Dozens become hundreds. I pass evenings listening to true crime podcasts or half-watching *Tiger King* on Netflix, and sewing, pressing, pleating, pinning, cutting. I wear a mask while I do it, but still I catch a hint of some animal scent from my sewing machine. Oil gone rancid in the gears, probably, or spools of flea market thread pissed on by some cat, or just my own human odor, the smell of my own woven breath. Masks soak in my sink. Tumble in my dryer. They will cover so many mouths. Sewists in this growing group trade fabric. Hunt for hard-to-find elastic. A hush-hush truck backs into an alley and we cheer, pick up our stretchy rations stuffed into paper lunch bags, which no one needs for lunch anymore.

Sometimes, I resist an urge to wear all of the completed masks at once. Just for the excess. And I recall a time when my five-year-old pulled on ten underwear as a joke. I think of the book *Caps for*

Sale, where the peddler carries his entire inventory atop his head. Oh and that one winter, when my husband wore all of his sweaters, just to make me smile. Just to have me peel them off.

If you gathered, did you forget your Daily Wellness? Did you mask your forget?

We have been meticulous in our quarantine to prepare for a beach vacation with my aging parents. On the drive, we stop to pee in the woods, won't enter a restroom. But within hours of arrival at the coast, my father has a non-Covid medical crisis and we are inside the local hospital Emergency Department, where our charge nurse tells us we share a wall with a Covid patient. Through my mask, I smell disinfectant in the air. I smell the doctor's shampoo. I wonder about the virus: shampoo ratio moving through the vents. When they begin to remove my father's clothes, I step into the hall.

It's a quiet night for the staff here. There are empty triage rooms. But I can hear at least two patients coughing. The one next door sounds like a young man. Another, down the hall, sounds like a kid. I overhear a nurse on the phone. She's discussing an 8-year-old with poor oxygen levels. Maybe it's Covid. Maybe it's some other, heavy, unmoving affliction. I call my sister, a nurse herself, give her the update. My muffled, masked chatter mixes with the sounds of the lobby. The coughing behind doors, the clicking of keyboards, flush of some toilet. The single ring of the phone, the nurse's *Hello?*, a question she asks over and over. Now the cry of a baby in the lobby, now a pen clicked to write, a file dropped, carbon copies spilling out, pastels, and I can hear that the floor where they land is gritty and I can hear someone far away asking *Can I help you?* the first way and I can hear my father, now decent, calling out *Okay! Okay!* Which I take to mean *Marianne, come back inside. Stay with me now.*

If you gathered, do you prefer not to answer?

A friend who was drifting away before quarantine drifts even further. But one afternoon, Melissa walks by my house with her kids when I happen to be out on the lawn. As if summoned, my kids emerge, and the children are circling one another. Their bodies remember pouncing. Months back, they would have called themselves best friends. But now it is strange. I want to tell her that my kids draw her kids in their drawings, that her kids have rooms in the oceanside treehouse mine plan to inhabit as adults. I can't get the words out.

Though it is a sunny day, the kids find two umbrellas hanging from the stroller she's parked in the grass. They use them as shields. They use them as swords but only against the dangerous air. *My kids might break your umbrellas,* I say. Melissa says they are already halfway broken. Eventually, the weapons are abandoned and we follow the kids as they dash to the backyard, the backyard where they always used to play. And they play. We have a swing now. We have new, challenging obstacles to climb. They are okay. We are okay. Later, we text that *it was so nice.* So so so nice nice nice. Which means, I thought it would feel worse than that.

If you prefer not to answer, do you prefer your symptoms?

My boys and I capture Pokémon characters in the Miller Park woods. *Don't run with my phone!* I call to them as they run ahead with my phone, which guides the game. There's a Charmander by the baseball field. An Espeon at the creekside shelter. I fail to see the appeal of collecting these characters, of forcing them into battle. *They like it!* The boys tell me, when I ask if Espeon might prefer to be free. But then, my kids like to be captured, too, are still little enough that they ask me to chase them. They find comfort in the sensation of running their hardest away and knowing I am on their heels, impossible to lose.

When we are ready to head home, we hear a mother screaming on the playground, where ribbons of caution tape dance in the wind. *Stop, Peter! Peter, stop! Stop!* She holds an infant in her arms, behind the fence. She is trying to open the gate but it's a tricky one if you haven't done it before, child-proof. Beyond the fence, beyond her reach, is Peter, a tiny toddler, clumsily making his way down a steep stone staircase. Peter ignores her completely, utterly focused on the challenge of his unsteady body. He's a genius, for a minute. I get to Peter easily. Normally I would pick the child up, deliver him to his mother. But I don't have a mask and I don't want to get too close. So I hover at his side and walk down with him, ready to catch him if he falls. I will hold him only when the danger of not holding him feels higher than the danger of holding.

Later that spring, I hike with a friend along a river. A river I used to live beside. A river flowing with life and runoff, fish and PFAS. My friend has a phobia of snakes, and so naturally we come upon a snake. Venomous. It is physiologically impossible for her to cross its path, which she needs to do in order to leave the woods. So she will have to stay here, on the riverbank, forever. She is imagining her new life already, the excellent view. I give her some pep talk and then grab her hand and run, pulling her past the snake, who doesn't lunge for us, who doesn't even register our presence. We map our wonder. River. Snake. Sky. The song of the water. Our birdy shrieks, when I grabbed her hand and forgot, briefly, the risk.

If you gathered, did you gather outdoors? If you prefer not to answer, did you gather indoors?

The game is called Midnight Chase, though it is only 8 p.m. Labor Day weekend. Six adults drink on the deck. Six kids run around in the dark with water cannons, giddy to play with someone other than their siblings. Case numbers are fairly low and we're staying outdoors. None of our work puts us much at risk, and the kids have kept mostly home. We have all the reasons. We say them over and over. I drink too much, too fast. White wine. I'm unsteady when I walk down the stairs to sit by the fire. The kids scream when they find one another in the dark, when they are found. When is the last time I have screamed like that? Sheer terror and thrill, no thought of the neighbors, just the body announcing itself as wholly alive, even as it faces a weapon, a zombie, an unmasked child halfway up the branches of the magnolia tree, close enough to midnight for a seven-year-old. Even as I savor this company, this energy, I doubt our indulgence. When I toast a marshmallow, I burn it, as if that will purify everything else we've consumed tonight. The meal, the love, the air we share, the air the kids trap in glass jars when the fireflies dance, no worry that they will be taken if they dare to glow.

Months later, I get an invitation from a very distant acquaintance, to meet in a field in Kernersville with other women, and scream into the darkness. *Sounds amazing*, I text, but I do not go.

Did one or more persons undergo?

My 80-year-old father is a volunteer history teacher at a tiny Catholic high school. He teaches in person, masked, and won't be talked out of it, though my mother has tried. The weather is cooling, but we drive two hours to Asheville to sit outdoors and visit. We wear masks, but my mother is hard of hearing. I repeatedly remove my mask to yell summaries of the conversation: the classes I'm teaching, the Christmas requests the kids plan to send to Santa wink wink wink wink wink wink. It is a short visit. Dad grows dizzy, Mom gets restless. We leave them with a paper plate of pumpkin muffins tucked under aluminum foil.

My mother wants to know if the muffins have any ingredients that she's allergic to. *Gluten? Peanuts? Walnuts? Any banana in there? Is this a mix, Marianne?*

I assure her that I made them from scratch. In my 39 years I haven't poisoned her yet.

Oats? she asks. *Almonds?*

Did you wash your immediate household?

Zero percent carbon monoxide. That's what I like to see. Some houses I test have 60, 70 percent. We've called the furnace technician not because of carbon monoxide but because of some peeling liner I noticed in one of our heat vents. Our house was built in the '30s and I don't take any chances when wires fray, paint chips, or mysterious substances slough off into blowing hot air. He hasn't any clue what's peeling or if it might be toxic, but he is excited about our furnace, which is over 20 years old, ancient by his standards. In my kitchen, while the CO monitor monitors, he steps close to show me his phone, where he has recorded a video of our antique furnace—the blaze inside, the door dropping open—to send to his friends. It feels oddly intimate, this footage he's collected, our home's metal, sexy secret. It feels transgressive, the way he keeps it like some cheap souvenir.

Meanwhile, I've ordered my kids to stay outside or upstairs while he does his thing. They are wild and uncooperative, and my parenting turns ugly, furrowed brow and screen time bribery. The tech takes his sweet time gathering his things. And I don't want to parent in front of him. I don't want to chat with him about how crazy the world is, not inside my home, not while we watch my fire on his phone. I don't want to hear his opinion on whether or not I should trust the vaccines that are proving to be 90% effective. 95% effective. I just want to know what's disintegrating in my air vents, if it's coating our lungs in invisible glitter, if it's going to kill us. He says he will look into it. Says he will get back to me. And we both know he is full of shit.

If you gathered your hands, did one or more persons outside of your immediate household gather their hands?

I drive north to a strip mall in Surry County, where I'm volunteering to monitor the processing of absentee ballots for our general election. It is unglamorous work. I'm to observe for several hours and keep close track of any rejected or controversial ballots. There are none, and the slightest question around a single ballot leads to thoughtful consideration by bipartisan members of the Board of Elections, who unanimously agree that the vote is valid. The process is boringly functional and fair.

One member of the BOE is participating remotely, and I eventually glean that he has been exposed to Covid. I also know that he was in this very room, with these very people, just last night. Breathing, counting. My anxiety gets the best of me and I leave the meeting, resume my observation online when I get home. When I log into Zoom, they are on a break. One representative removes his mask to eat what looks like chicken salad with a plastic fork. Before him, a single-serve bag of potato chips sits, unopened, on the conference table. What can it hold, twelve, thirteen potato chips? Fourteen, fifteen? The bag is round with air, full of promise, but he never tears it open.

Overall, did you gather your symptoms?

I'm nearly forty, which means many of my friends are forty, which means that midlife crises are cropping up like mushrooms after a rain. At a backyard fire pit, a friend updates me on the shifting boundaries of her marriage. How isolation has been an incubator for upheaval. Another friend quits her job with a flourish, no backup plan. Another abandons her art, buys all the things, packs shiny purchases around her like bubble wrap. She's the art now. We are all longing for an ending; we will end anything in reach just to prove that endings are still real.

To maintain social distance, I sit too far from the fire to feel its heat. But there is the light, at least. The happy flames, the corners they brighten, the shadows they cast. Friends turn to me, wanting to know what's new with me, that is, what in my life is almost over.

Did outside your immediate household undergo one or more persons?

Crick finds me in the backyard. I'm masked, with my sister, watching the kids play. Some running game. Everybody seems to be It. The air is cold, it's nearly Christmas. I sip echinacea tea to stay warm, burn the roof of my mouth. Crick is a pediatric emergency physician. He treated Nolan when he turned blue. He's seen me frantic, sobbing. His folks live next door but are away. Checking on their house, he has found a misdelivered package. He hands it to me and it is decidedly heavy, addressed to my husband. I remember that Rob ordered something on Amazon and told me *Don't look it up!* I take a guess. There was this gadgety back-massager a friend had recommended and I had put it on my wish list. A wish list that I loathe. A list that goes on and on and on and on and on and on. Twin pangs. One, appreciation for my not-good-at-gifting husband for rooting around this wish list and finding something that might ease some of my stress. Two, a heart-deadening realization that I am a woman who will open a gadget on Christmas.

Crick and I oblige, *How are you?* The question feels absurd. How is anyone, sourdough starters notwithstanding? But Crick tells me that he just got the first dose of the vaccine. I want to rush him with a hug, but I don't. I have never hugged him. I barely know him. But he is hope with limbs right now. He is real and injected. I introduce my sister and feel proud that we are following the rules, that the kids are masked, too, that we're a handful of people whose lives he won't have to save tonight.

On Christmas, I lift the heavy gift into my lap and tear the paper.

Turns out, it is not the Zyllion Shiatsu Back and Neck Massager—Kneading Massage Pillow with Heat for Shoulders, Lower Back, Calf. It is a set of six ivory pillar candles, the only thing we can burn in our shallow fireplace. So here's the man I love, his own piano hands on my Shoulders, Lower Back, Calf. Here's the reminder that even this dark winter can be lit with a match.

If you wore a mask, did the mask mask?

One day in early January, my Daily Wellness Survey comes with an extra set of questions, designed to monitor the impact of the holidays on the spread of the pandemic. *Between December 18th and January 3rd, did you gather with one or more persons outside of your immediate household? If you gathered, did you wear a mask? If you gathered, did you gather outdoors?* The questions go on and on and on and on but they are all the same question. *How alone are you?*

A few hours after I answer this expanded survey, there is an attempted coup at the nation's Capitol. I'm on a Zoom meeting at the time, until my colleagues and I realize what is happening, turn sick about it, log out, watch in horror on our ever-open news tabs. And while this mob violence, this white supremacy, giddy and hungry, is an absolute terror, I know that some part of my shock is the same that I feel when watching crowd scenes in pre-Covid movies. Here, a dance. There, a war. It has become bizarre to see so many people so close and sometimes I call out, in earnest, *Six feet, Natalie Portman! Where is your mask, Bradley Cooper?* I feel a reflex of protection for every actor, not only the outmanned police and elected officials, cowering in their chambers, but also for the shirtless QAnon guy wearing an animal pelt. The masked figure clutching a Bible with hands clad in skeleton gloves. The blonde in red with the sign *THE CHILDREN CALL OUT FOR JUSTICE.* She is on her phone. Maybe with her children. Maybe they are really chanting *JUSTICE, JUSTICE, JUSTICE.* Or maybe they are only asking,

When are you coming home? Mom, where are you?

If you wore a mask, was your mask a flag?

Proud Boys. A man who goes by Milkshake. What do you love more than love? Oath Keepers. A man in an eye patch who says, *My only regret is they should have brought rifles. We should have brought rifles. We could have fixed it right then and there.*

If your mask was a flag, did you burn it with your breath?

Hush-hush. It is cold enough to see your breath. Four figures, early morning, haul lumber across the Capitol lawn. To build a gallows. Can I help you? To hang an orange noose.

If your breath was short, was it because you were running?

A senator raises a fist in solidarity with the rioters, riles them up. Birdy shrieks. Sounds amazing. Later, and lightly, he runs from them, through the hallways of the Capitol building, down a staircase. He carries a tidy folder and wears a crisp blue medical mask. Outside, rioters scale walls, smash windows.

If your breath was short, was it because you were beating a man?

Officer Michael Fanone: dragged, beaten, tased. Suffered brain injuries, a heart attack, and burns.

If you were beating a man, were you using a crutch or a fire extinguisher or your own two hands?

Officer Brian Sicknick, pepper-sprayed, two strokes.
Officer Jeffrey Smith, suicide.

Officer Howard Liebengood, suicide.

What blunt force trauma does to the brain. Every other muscle from toes to scalp shouting, And me. And me. And me. And me.

Did you draw blood?

A rioter, Kevin Greeson, drops dead of a heart attack while on the phone with his wife. Another, Benjamin Phillips, dies of a stroke. He's a computer programmer with a side hustle selling patriotic stuffed kangaroos at Trump events. Souvenirs. He has brought his entire inventory. These *Trumparoo* kangaroos wear red neckties. They boast a whorl of Trumpy hair. Their eyes are open, lucky-lashed. They have pouches, in which they carry baby kangaroos. Which means they are mothers. Male kangaroos do not have pouches. Male kangaroos are bad at carrying.

Was the blood a test?

An officer shoots a rioter, Ashli Babbitt, as she climbs through an open window, a Trump flag tied around her neck. Blood pours from the hole of her mouth, the last thing she will ever say. She's the art now.

Was the test healthy?

The rioters gather closer and closer. Rosanne Boyland is crushed to death by this closeness. Unprecedented, impossible to breathe closeness.

Was the experience close?

Hours too late, Trump encourages the rioters to go home. He tells them, *I know your pain. I know your hurt. . . . We love you. You're very special. . . . I know how you feel.* He wears a red necktie. He has no discernible pouch, but there is a mob for him, always a mob for him, *CALLING OUT FOR JUSTICE,* clamoring to be held.

If you gathered, did you gather the broken glass?

Are there still shards in the soles of your boots?

Do they still catch the sunlight?

Do they

How do I ask this?

Do they make you less alone?

THIS IS THE OCEAN AND THIS IS YOU

W hen a hurricane is in the cards, some vacationers stay put. The mothers study the bones of their rental houses and deem them structurally sound. They eyeball the ocean at high tide. Still far enough away. The children dutifully eat all of the popsicles in preparation for the power outage, and the fathers drag their camp chairs to the cottage rooftops, prop them open, crack some beers, and holler at the wind until their wives shout that enough is enough, come down here and grill these burgers before they turn.

Other families will flee the coast when instructed by local authorities. These are the vacationers who plan for probable disasters, whose fathers fill up the gas tanks first thing in the morning, whose children own exactly two swimsuits apiece, no excess, whose mothers are the type to keep a small but sufficient Go Bag.

Of course, you have those that hem and haw until the lights flicker. But in time they'll toss up their hands and say *okay, fine, let's just go,* leaving a light on, forgetting the towels looping in the dryer. And just up the beach from that family are nine redheaded Irish Catholics who constitute the last family to evacuate Wells Beach, Maine, in the summer of 1991. That would be my family, the Uphams, ferrying suitcases and tote bags to a Nissan Stanza and a Buick Roadmaster, fleeing Hurricane Bob.

Whether we are actually the last or not is unknown, but the news reporter sees it that way. In her yellow poncho, she flags us down, gets my teenaged sister to crank down the driver's side window of the Stanza. The microphone is veiled with a plastic bag; the sky empties itself as the women lean in close for several minutes. Only one moment makes it onto the evening news, which we watch in a questionable motel room a few hours later. When asked, through building wind, *Why did you wait so long to leave?* Kathryn shouts, with a laugh, *Stupidity!*

Seated on the stained duvets, we smirk. We know what she means. That we could have left hours earlier, and found a nicer hotel, and a table at an adequate restaurant, and just been normal and perfect and invisible and un-interviewed if it wasn't for our insufferable mother.

We didn't wait so long to leave. It's just that leaving, for my family, wasn't a discrete event. It required preparation, imagination, fortitude, and do-overs. It required breaks, sometimes naps. Before a previous summer trip to the coast, we'd waited on the couch in our Keds for several hours before our mother declared it was all just too much, and we would try again the following afternoon. And it was too much. Nine winter coats just in case. Every ointment known to man. We rolled our eyes. We brought our index fingers to our temples and wound them around and around to add to our shared mental Rolodex of crazy mother transgressions. Forbidding haircuts until we mashed gum into our braids, on purpose. Forbidding gum. Stacking *PennySavers* in the bathroom, *Poughkeepsie Journals* on the couches, keeping years of *Yellow Pages* in case, as my brother once said, we needed to call the past. Fearing bears enough to get a gun. Fearing bees enough to build a garage so she could get to her car without stepping outside. We didn't say OCD or anxiety or depression or any of the other diagnoses that might have applied had she found help. We said crazy. Crazy was easy.

Still, we didn't always know what counted as remarkable. Some of us were teenagers before we realized that every load of laundry did not, in fact, require two complete cycles in the washing machine. That *putting the clothes through a rinse* was not a thing our peers had ever heard of. That a third *rinse-rinse* was not required if the twice-washed clothes held any lingering aroma of detergent. We knew other mothers could be particular. One might lick her fingertips to fix her child's hair. One might ration sugar, go overboard during science fair season. Ours would drop us off at school, then circle back around the lot to be sure she hadn't, inadvertently, killed one of our classmates on her first pass.

In the case of Hurricane Bob, it was not the storm that swept up her attention, for she was rarely unmoored by actual crises. She kept calm through our concussions, her cancer, the global pandemic which simply validated her theory that stepping through the door wasn't worth the trouble. She was a nurse, top of her class at Columbia, often the most levelheaded of any of us when it counted. We saw no wave of panic about Bob or the safety of her children. We saw a desperate rescue of the nearly empty sunscreens, the back-up plastic bags. We shimmied under beds to prove they were clear, checked every drawer, over and over. Every fold in every towel, her way. It took forever. She took forever. Then she made all of us use the dingy bathroom, even my father. *I don't care if it's two drops!* Stepping outdoors, she seemed surprised to find that the world was wet, windy, darkening. That the weather hadn't waited. She took forever getting into the car, forever buckling her seatbelt, forever arranging her enormous purse in the lap of whatever child was stuck in the front middle seat. That purse, she would say *pocketbook*, strained at the seams. *Hold this*, Mom would say. If you needed something, she had it in there somewhere, was her point.

Almost three decades later, several weeks into Covid-19 isolation, I kiss my boys goodnight and tuck myself into bed with a book on climate change, *The Story of More* by Hope Jahren. In chapter five, she asks, *If your world ever falls apart, and you lose everything, where is the place that you will turn to, and then return to?* Jahren summons her childhood home but mine—a one-story in the woods of Pawling, NY—is not my haven. And it's not because the house sold last year, or that New York is faring far worse with the pandemic than my city in North Carolina. It's that I can feel no tide, no pull to return to a home I spent years preparing to leave. To leave the depression and the phobias and the rage, to somehow unweather them. To abandon those hilltop storms, dazzling and deafening and always ending with a blown transformer, the electric pump to our well rendered useless. So what if my mother had the foresight to fill the bathtub and the spaghetti pot in preparation? It didn't, at the time, feel like love because she'd fill the same bathtub no matter the forecast, and we didn't know what to do with a bathtub of stale water, dust accumulating on its surface. We wanted it fresh, from the tap, in a glass. Also she discouraged glass. Breakable. Taking up valuable dishwasher real estate. She preferred us to use disposable Dixie cups, to then rinse them and throw them away nested inside one another. *They should make a telescope*, she'd say, and we would oblige, even adjusting the trash of our siblings if they had thrown it away wrong. Until, one by one, we were gone. Gone to college, marriage, therapy, religion, poetry, anxiety, or Texas. So to where will I turn? I consider the possibility that I am now, today, living in that place of comfort and stability to which I'm supposed to flee in case of disaster. Maybe that's true. How lucky. And also troubling because if so, there is nowhere to go.

A day or two later, though, a different home surfaces. That rental house at Wells Beach. It wasn't ours. It belonged to our neighbors, John and Fayne Lappas, owners of the local grocery who gave many of us our first jobs. They had a daughter who was into horses, another who died of lupus, and a buoyant, attractive son who occasionally jogged by our house, shirtless. We must have gotten a deal on the rental, which was nothing fancy. Wood paneling from top to bottom. A tiny, temperamental television where we'd watched footage of the Iraqi invasion of Kuwait the summer before Bob. The house had a deck made of splinters, double beds full of sand and too many bodies and not enough blankets. But it was on the beach so who cared? Inhabiting the house wasn't the point. We spent our days near it, getting sunburned, collecting rocks, eating Now and Laters at the arcade, and freezing to death in the ocean, letting it knock us around into the sort of abandon we imagined other kids could feel on land.

The image of the house that comes to mind does not contain me. It's the one from the evening news. The crew filmed it from the street. It looks small and unremarkable, and the fog obscures the ocean. There might be any landscape on the other side. It's our house but not our house. Our family as framed by a stranger. My sister but with exaggerated features. Her hair is extra ginger against the gray sky, her laugh damp, soprano, unkind in a way I'd never heard as unkind.

And where is my mother? In the motel bathroom, perhaps, lining up nine toothbrushes, or stacking the rolls of toilet paper she insisted we swipe from the house. She's fidgeting with the room's cooling system, noting the scent of mildew, not minding the noise of the fan, which softens her children's harsh voices. Through the window, she sees that my father has parked her Buick where she asked, within sight, a stone's throw. But has he locked it? Out the door she goes, umbrella ready. She passes an ice station, an out-of-order vending machine. She descends two concrete flights of stairs, avoids the railing because of germs. In the lot, in the rain, she checks every door. Locked. She is surprised and satisfied with my father's thoroughness, satisfied with her own. Does she take a moment now, to be alone? The way I do when my own kids are in bed and I'm out front on the sidewalk, dragging our recycling bin into place for tomorrow's pickup? Does she marvel at the sweet evening air, the way the rain washes away some invisible accumulation? Does she forgive her own mother, who also had a heavy mind? Does she forgive us, her small and mean sons and daughters?

It makes no sense to flee one disaster for another, to imagine refuge in a hurricane. But Bob gave us a kicked up breeze, the thrill of possibility, as we fled him. He gave us a taste of electricity in the gathering clouds. We could have been any well-equipped family caravanning inland. We could have been grateful for any motel, any place that would take us, any dry bed, any crackling television program, any loving and difficult parent. We weren't but we could have been. We fled Bob, together. We had what we needed to survive, including a mother to whom we could truthfully say, *You thought of everything*.

We fall asleep thinking this is it. The end of summer. When the storm clears, we'll head home, bound for Trapper Keepers and paper grocery bags cut into textbook covers. Back to sibling dispersal, our feisty raft untied, each of us doomed to a different classroom full of girls who soaked their hair in Sun-In, of boys who'd outgrown whatever small pathetic game we had only just discovered. Back to plaid skirts, chicken-on-a-bun, and Please Excuse My Dear Aunt Sally. That order of operations, the mnemonic that we were to summon when solving overwhelming equations. Parentheses first. Then Exponents. Multiply. Divide. Add. Subtract. And what was Aunt Sally's transgression? For what were we apologizing? Was it this list of directions, her quirky mathematical demands? Or was the order of operations the remedy for Aunt Sally, the tonic that would cure her behavior, would soothe her beleaguered relatives. Their rolled eyes. Their sighs of exasperation, regular as ocean waves. The sound of the tide blaming the moon.

My mother, nearly 80, is likely fixed in her orbit. She will not give up her many rituals, piles, and checklists, although she never bothered to make one for the big family beach trip she was slated to join this summer. She had plenty of reasons to cancel. She's been in terrible back pain, with a crushed vertebra, bone turned to sand, still healing. She struggles with stairs and despises the heat. My father finds travel difficult, too. But her main reason, she tells me, is that she can't bear to pack for the journey. And there is no packing *for* her, no rushing her along, we gave up those fantasies long ago. In fact, we no longer mind how long it takes to put fresh sheets on a bed when we visit, Mom standing beside us, instructing us through every hospital corner as if we've forgotten the order. Every chore, even those she only supervises, leaves her totally, utterly exhausted. So packing for the beach? *It's just too much, Marianne*, she says. And my answer is easy and true, *I know, Mom. I'm sorry. And we will miss you.*

As it happens, summer isn't over. Bob wallops Massachusetts, Connecticut, and Rhode Island but peters out in Maine. We are allowed to return to Wells to finish our vacation. And it is strange to come back, to be granted a do-over for something we feel we did adequately well the first time around. When we return, we find that Bob's landfall has left a pile of sand at our doorstep, dead fish drying up where we'd played. But the house itself seems untouched and while we have never been terribly concerned about its fate—it isn't ours—we find ourselves grateful, uncharacteristically lucky. We dump our bags on the unmade beds, dig out our suits and Walkmans, congregate outside. We throw stones into waves and wander up and down the shore, looking for obvious damage. Finding none, we lounge, dig, burn, float.

This is the ocean and this is you, I tell my boys. We're at Topsail Island and I'm trying to explain to them how every wave tugs them down the coast, away from our buckets and cooler and canopy. Away from me. They appear to listen, to nod at my nonsensical hand gestures. But when they play I see no evidence that they care, or even notice where their bodies are going. They'll meet any wave where it crashes. *Okay*, I say a little while later. *Just, every once in a while, find me on the beach, and come all the way back*. And when they turn to wave, or brag, or simply want to fix their eyes on me for a beat, I wave back, or blow kisses, or embarrass them with a jaunty dance, my body soft, pale, loose. And sometimes my throat tightens and I stand up to coax them back. I sweep my arms dramatically, the way my mother would when I was small. The way a witch reverses a foolish curse. The way a weatherman shows us all of the places where the sky is about to fall.

THE LARK

The crested lark was the first bird to be created, even before Gaia,
the Earth.

The Lark and Her Crest, Aesop's Fables

First, there is a bird in flight. She has nowhere to land because there is no land. Earth does not yet exist. She wonders if this is an error of creation or the aim of creation. She would ask her father, but he is dead.

How the lark recognizes death, when nothing has ever died, Aesop fails to say. Maybe she's heard stories of Earth, just as we've heard stories of Heaven. Maybe her father warned her. Or maybe it's pure instinct when she readies his body for burial, though burial is impossible. There is no dirt, nothing to shovel, no sheets of moss to drape over him, no branches to cover the spot, no stone to mark it.

Five days pass. The father grows heavy. The daughter searches in vain for a place to set him down. In her embrace, his body turns sour. So she does what she must. She buries her father in her head.

(   )

I know my father is dying before he does. I have no gift of premonition. I just learn it first. It all happens in the wrong order. Cancer, of course. Glioblastoma. A tumor in his head. Inoperable. Three or four months, tops. I'm told to keep it from him until the biopsy confirms it, to be the chirpy daughter he expects.

Hey, I say, entering his hospital room. *All this to get out of book club?*

He laughs. They're reading something he doesn't care for. Something *emotional* by a Southern writer. The group consists of mostly lilt-voiced women in soft cardigans and though my dad has lived in North Carolina for a few years, Paul Upham remains a hopeless, lonely Yankee, cringing his way through stories about crawdads and quilt circles, wishing for a weighty biography of a just man in a just war.

All day I am cheerful and steady. I fetch snacks and pillows, savor his old stories, and click through every TV channel until we find *NCIS.* He needs my help in the bathroom and it's a big, tragic deal that first time. When he naps, I text my brother. *I feel nothing inside.* Empty, but not emptied.

( )

I'm not a bird person. I don't know a lark from a wren from a house finch. I was raised to see nature as something outside, beyond, not mine.

Though we lived in the woods, we weren't at home in the woods. It was simply a house my folks could afford: a one-story ranch on what is informally known as Little Purgatory Hill, the hill next to Purgatory Hill, where Washington's troops fell ill one winter. My folks were city people, and when they moved into the house, my mother hung an unlicensed rifle on the wall of the basement, for fear of bears. When the bees became untenable, she spent the savings on an attached garage so that she could move from house to car without setting foot outdoors. When a bat took flight in our dining room, my father battled it with a broom rather than open a window. He showed us the body, less disgusting than we guessed, and then banished us from the room for several months. Because bats carry disease.

And the mosquitoes, don't get my mother started, the mosquitoes were enough to *drive her to drink,* though she never drank more than a sip of Communion wine. She was unapologetically wistful for the days of DDT. *Just a little* she would say *would go a long way.* She knew of its disastrous effects on the environment, the brittle bird eggs, the poisoned fish, but she held only affection for her child-hood memories of chasing the low-flying planes as they sprayed the suburbs of Boston. They sprayed for the mosquitoes but also, for almost a decade, because they mistakenly guessed it might prevent the spread of polio, my parents' first pandemic.

It is probably not a pesticide, but an herbicide, which gives both of my parents cancer. My mother gets it first, a rare soft tissue sarcoma in the walls of her uterus, an affront to a woman who birthed seven children and carried more. When she is diagnosed, I am pregnant with her fourteenth grandchild. She survives, her feather-cut hair in clumps in her hands. Ten years later, my father, the glioblastoma. Highly aggressive. A cancer that can double in size in seven weeks. By the time they find it, it is the size of a chicken egg, nesting in his frontal lobe, messing with his cognitive function. Within a month, he is paraplegic.

The herbicide still active in my parents' bodies, fifty years after exposure, is Agent Orange. A notorious poison in Vietnam and East Asia, the defoliant was used to strip the Earth of her leafy vines, force enemies into sight. Agent Orange, named as such because the barrels were marked with an orange ring around their middles, found my father when he was boots on the ground in Da Nang, but the chemical was also stored and sprayed on the island of Okinawa, where my mother served as a civilian nurse.

When, after two years, my dad came home, he was tasked with delivering the news of fallen soldiers to their loved ones. In the memories he records in his later years, he writes,

They are each etched in memory. One mother's son died as a Navy

corpsman (medic with the Marines), serving on patrol in the jungle.

(These medics were prime targets. Kill a medic, kill whichever sol-diers that medic might have been able to save. He goes on:)

> *She was an elderly widow living alone in a poor tenement on the south side of New Bedford. There were no relatives. When her door opened, over her shoulder, I spotted a shrine to her son, covered with letters and pictures from him and other mementos. The English language is not adequate to describe her feelings or mine.*

Language is not adequate. But it's a bit of soil, a place to land.

(   )

Many of *Aesop's Fables* are not, well, fables. In ancient times, *The Lark and Her Crest* offered no fixed moral lesson. It was an etiological tale. It wasn't until the late 1800s that Reverend George Fyler Townsend, a British translator, told us what it should mean, pinning a moral to the end, the tale's own little headstone: *Youth's first duty is reverence to parents.* I shrug at this. Easy enough for the lark. In a world of endless Sky, there is nowhere else for reverence to go.

What captivates me is the image of the bird opening up her skull, as one opens a suitcase, to welcome the physical wreckage of death. What she keeps is not a memory or an emotion. It's a body, rotting. Bones, feathers, organs, the talons, the beak. It is a rejection of metaphor. It is a stark love that refuses to separate promise from ruin, new down from blight.

I was not raised on Aesop, though I'm familiar with the classics. I think I know what they mean. When my five-year-old son plays with fabrication, I even attempt to use *The Boy Who Cried Wolf* to make a point about honesty. In Aesop's version, the wolf kills a flock of sheep the boy is tending. In my version, the horrible version I stupidly tell my son, the wolf kills the boy. I forget there should be sheep. I become the wolf.

When I see the wrong story taking hold, I try to untell it. I tell my son to forget the fable, that little kids shouldn't be on wolf patrol anyway. He says maybe the boy thought there really was a wolf, that he was afraid. And I say yes, fear can be as real as any animal. Maybe the boy was telling the truth.

While today the fables often take the form of children's books, their early usage favored political rhetoric, moral philosophy, and the coded sharing of slave narratives (Aesop is said to have once been a slave). As with *The Crested Lark*, many of the fables lacked a single lesson. As the stories migrated their way from all over the globe, and were collected and attributed to Aesop, morals were attached or inserted to suit the storyteller's purpose. As a result, some of the fables contain multiple morals and can be downright contradictory. Take *The Two Men, the Eagle, and the Fox* (#275). In one translation, we're told to cozy up to those who harm us (an *enemies closer* philosophy). At the same time, we're told to simply avoid these *evil-doers* altogether, saving our affection for those who have treated us with care.

This affection, this reverence, Aesop tells us, is owed not only to humans and animals, but to the Earth itself. In *The Deer and the Vine* (#77), a deer hides from a hunter in the generous leaves of a grapevine. Time passes, dulling her fear, sharpening her appetite. Thinking herself safe, the deer tastes the very leaves that have saved her. She wolfs them down, stripping the vine and revealing herself to the patient, lingering hunter, who takes easy aim.

(   )

My father was, by his own admission, a terrible shot. He never fired at anybody, but many fired at him as he flew into Da Nang in 1965. He was weeks late to his post. He writes:

Since the flagship carried nuclear weapons, its course was highly classified. My Top Secret security clearance was "lost at sea" in the military bureaucracy and no one could or would confirm the ship's location. So I "skylarked" from Boston to San Francisco . . . to Tokyo . . . to Manila . . . and finally landed in Vietnam; a cumulative dillydally of over a month getting to my first command. I found those "unexplored countries" (Hamlet?) fascinating and delightful.

The Hamlet reference is typical of my dad. He prided himself on being well-read, and his unfinished notes are full of these buried parentheticals he'd hoped to cross-check and develop later. In considering the etymology of Operation Rolling Thunder, he ventured, *perhaps a Freudian-slip blasphemy lifted from the Christian hymn, O Store Gud. How Great Thou Art. (American Manicheism/Manifest Destiny/Imperialism).*

In describing his fascination with the sea, he names an *insatiable curiosity about what lay over and beyond the horizon, a fascination with unknown places and futures. (Here insert Proust's Remembrance etc. re invoking childhood memories, or Freud's dreams interpretation of childhood desires, or Masefield, or Thucydides or Melville or Kon Tiki or Nautilus or Plato's Atlantis).*

You know. One of those.

Meanwhile, the spraying of Agent Orange was well underway. Over nine years, the US military would spray upwards of eleven million gallons of the poison, along with another eight million gallons of other so-called *Rainbow Herbicides* including Agents White, Pink, Purple, Blue, and Green. To a far lesser extent, the dioxins were also sprayed, tested, or stored in the Philippines, Cambodia, Canada, India, Johnston Atoll, Korea, Laos, Thailand, and twelve US states. Some of the damage was immediate—crops withered, skin burned, nerves misfired. Pregnant women woke to blood in the bed, pressed their hands to their bellies, feeling, in vain, for movement. Much of the impact unfolded—continues to unfold—in the months and years after exposure. Hundreds of thousands of children and grandchildren born with debilitating and painful birth defects. Immune suppression. Diabetes. Skin lesions. Cancers. Malformed hearts. Dioxins buried, still, in the bodies of fish and bugs and birds, in water and soil.

The unofficial motto of this campaign was a riff on Smokey Bear, known of course for the line, *Only YOU can prevent a forest fire.* As they doused the earth with a different kind of burn, one they believed they were somehow immune to, American soldiers joked, *Only you can prevent a forest.*

( )

Here's something I'd like to unknow. When a body burns, say, in a crematorium, it adopts a posture known as the *pugilistic stance.* The connective tissue, tendons and ligaments, fascia and muscle, all of it desiccates in the heat, shrinks, shortens. The limbs fold in, the fingers curl into fists. The head lowers as if to protect itself. As the bones surface, the body resembles that of a boxer.

( )

The Agent Orange compensation eventually comes through. We find out at the funeral home, helping my mother initial her way through a mound of paperwork, and declining various commemorative add-ons (a necklace with my father's fingerprint before the prints disappear; a pricey, ugly ring that can hold a pinch of his ashes). My mother writes a check to pay for the burning of her husband's body and calls her bank to confirm her account balance. She's surprised to hear that she has plenty to cover it.

It's not a lot of money, but cold comfort is still comfort when you're living on Social Security and have drained your meager savings on end-of-life care. My father had always said, with pride, that he would spend his final days at the VA hospital, on the military's dime. But when the time came, the ambulance brought him to the wrong hospital, and the residual red tape paired with emergency

Covid policies meant that there was no bed for him. He landed in a private nursing home, where the staff was kind but stretched far too thin, where they forgot to cut up his food, where they couldn't respond to his call button in time to stop another bruising fall to the unforgiving floor. On visits, I'd wheel him into a little courtyard where one of the CNAs was working a side hustle, pinning freshly tie-dyed t-shirts onto the ornamental trees to dry in the sun. (My father, who had never worn tie-dye in his life, bought a few.) When Medicare stopped paying and the savings dwindled, my sister, a nurse, set up a hospital bed in her dining room and provided round-the-clock care for four months, her toddler tugging on one hand, my father's glass of thickened orange juice sweating in the other.

( )

As with the lark, my father's body remains uninterred for too long. Eleven days in the morgue, paperwork delayed at the VA, my father stored in some cold filing cabinet. It's so long that my mother asks me to ID the body again, to be sure he is still where we left him.

And as with the lark, he is not actually placed in the Earth. Instead, his urn is sealed several feet off the ground in a stone columbarium at the VA cemetery in Black Mountain. After *Taps* (moving) and a flag ceremony (awkward), my kids and their cousins wander among the headstones in the grass, more drawn to the graves that look like graves. They make a game of it: find the dead soldiers who share their names. There's Michael. There's Johnny. My siblings and I have differing opinions, or no opinions, on this behavior. But we find no energy for judgment. We observe the children as strangers, noting their delight at being together, which seems to have won out over their sadness at losing their grandfather, whom they never really knew. Just an old man who once schooled them in checkers, or told them, harshly, to keep their voices down.

( )

I have learned that when a lark builds a nest, she builds it in the ground. She knows it is a grave.

( )

During my father's final weeks, I dream. In one, I must carry him. We are in an anonymous neighborhood, where every house is the same. There is no way to mark space or time. He wears a hospital gown and hangs onto my back like a child. I tell him I can carry him for as long as he needs, and am surprised to hear myself say it and know that it is true.

In another dream, I'm looking out my window at my neighbor's bird feeder. It's winter in the dream and in real life and all sorts of birds are happy for the easy nourishment. A blue jay, I'm pretty sure. A cardinal. My grief already feels like a fully formed spinning planet, but my father is still alive. I hear his voice say, *Look to the birds*, even though I am already looking.

In another, he sits in his recliner, watching *Jeopardy!*. In life I'd keep score of his wins and wagers. He was good, his brain full of facts. Some nights, he'd treat himself to half a Bud Lite, nod off in his chair. In the dream, he leans forward and his back catches fire, big golden wings of flame. He shows no distress. My siblings and I gather around him to snuff out the flames with blankets which we seem to have kept for this purpose. There is relief until the fire returns. We use our bare hands, but they are not enough, and this time, the whole chair ignites. We drag the chair out into the yard, but I wake before the story ends.

( )

What is a bird? What is an angel? What is a pile of ash?

( )

Aesop doesn't actually say that the lark has to carry her father around for five days. He only says that the body *lied there, uninterred, for five days*. But where is *there?* If the world holds only Sky, then the lark herself is the only *there.* There is no Gaia, no celestial bodies, so there is no gravity tugging at wings, no risk of falling down. There is no down. She could simply hover beside her father forever, pretending they are separate.

( )

The avian *buried in the head* etiological motif is not unique to Aesop. Folklore scholars Yuri Berezkin and Evgeny Duvakin map how this image transcends geographic and temporal boundaries. In Western Asia, Umayya b. Abï-1-Salt, a contemporary of Muhammad, tells the story of the hoopoe who carries his mother's body through a rainstorm, finds no place to bury her, and buries her in his head. In North Africa, the hoopoe has a name—Hud-hud—and plenty of space to bury his mother, but the notion of ground burial is so upsetting that Hud-hud prefers to bury her in his head instead. For the Sorko people of Mali, head burial has little to do with grief, but is instead evidence of longevity, survival: the tiny tommifirri buries her mother in her head because, as the lark would tell you, the earth does not yet exist, and this is taken as proof that she is the eldest and wisest. In a similar tale from northern Liberia, the hornbill cries, *Look at my head! Do you not see my mother's coffin there?*

Then there is the Wayao tale, *The Man Who Didn't Go to Funerals,* in which the parent buries the child in his head. Here the parent is a human father who refuses to participate in the rituals of the dead, and so has failed to learn how to prepare the body or even where to find the burial grounds. *Eventually,* the story goes, *he becomes a hornbill bird with his strange beak and strange cry: "Where are the graves? Ku malembe, kwa-kwa-kwa?"*

( )

As the daughter of devout Catholics, the creation story that I have inherited opens The Book of Genesis, where the lark is not the first creation—birds are reserved for day five. Earth comes right away, although not as the dirt but as a *formless void* with *divine wind* until creation unfolds as a matter of separation, of un-burial. God divides the light from the darkness, the waters on land from the waters in heaven. He divides the sea from the land, the day from the night, invites plants and animals to spring forth from the soil and water, to multiply. Later, from dust, he pulls a man, then pulls the start of a woman clean out of the man's side. A world made whole in a week.

Pulling poison out of soil takes longer. Decades after Operation Ranch Hand, the US government found that the most effective process was thermal desorption, which entails creating a football field–sized tomb for the ruined earth. You heat the tomb to over 600 degrees Fahrenheit for several months, at which point most of the dioxin falls apart. Vaporization allows the remaining dioxin to be collected by vacuum, then shipped to a hazardous waste disposal site in Europe. The cooked, clean soil is then unburied and returned to the earth. The process is underway at Bien Hoa, the largest remaining hot spot in Vietnam, and should wrap up by 2030. When it happens, when the last shovelful is burned and tossed back into place, someone will say the story is over. Someone will wipe their brow and say, *There.* Even as Vietnamese children are born without eyes. Even as the Sky surrenders rain to fields full of life and unanswered questions. Even as veterans lay perfectly still on MRI tables, remembering the open burn pits in Iraq or Afghanistan, the pits where they lit up all the trash, from plastic water bottles to medical supplies, to entire Humvees, releasing endless plumes of toxic black smoke pitched Skyward.

( )

What am I forgetting? I try to locate myself among the handful of memories where I, one of seven children, had my father to myself, where we were the only two creatures in the world. There was the winter when only the two of us chose a Christmas tree from the church parking lot. The summer when I helped him haul the rusted air conditioner up from the basement and set it in the living room window so my mother could watch *Father Dowling Mysteries* in comfort. We took a handful of walks, a quarter mile down the dirt road to our mailbox, where he declared all of the mail *junk* and carried it home. Once, we walked on a beach as the weather shifted, carrying nothing. Once, a visit to the graves of his parents in Lynn. Never did I bury his feet in the sand. Never did I tuck a blanket around him until he was unable to do so himself.

( )

My father was a morning person, a lark, in a family of night owls. It is no surprise that he dies around 10 p.m. If he were still conscious, he might joke about being a real party animal, the first one to turn in. But he hasn't spoken in days. His last words, I believe, were a garbled *Thank you* to a hospice nurse who laid her hand on his heart and adjusted the angle of his bed.

I am with him at the end, only the two of us. His breathing is steady. *I'm going to the bathroom*, I tell him. *I'll stay here all night. But you don't have to.* I close a door between us. It's been an evening of murmuring and humming and playing ocean sounds through my phone, and when I flush, I am startled by the noise. I see my own alarm in the mirror, in the bright, bad light.

I remember a dream I had in pregnancy. I dreamed that morning sickness led me to throw up my unborn child. I had to fish him out of the swirling toilet water, had to swallow him back down so he could keep becoming whatever he was becoming.

When I open the door and return, my father is still. He looks unheld. Alone.

I've heard that sometimes the dying won't die until you accidentally let them go. You eat half a sandwich in the hall. You run to your car for a phone charger. Nature calls, and you listen. So here I am. Talons open, father gone forever. But then, from some deep solid place, his body remembers open air and he gulps it in, greedy. This happens a few times. And then it stops happening.

(   )

When we got to the end, I had expected to feel a shift in my heart or in my head. Instead, I sense arrival on my shoulders, a heavy creature, perched there. Not a metaphor. Not a lark, but something winged and warm and home. I exist, enough, to bear it. I understand that I am dying. This is what it is to be a parent, a child, a bird. To be soil, rich and new and ancient, and laced with what we've done.

I call my sister, interrupt her shower. She arrives with wet hair to die along with me. To tend to our father's bluing body.

When the undertaker zips him into a bag, our tears flow. We cast about for tissues, as if we haven't been crying all week. We find none. No tissues at a deathbed. Have we imagined them all this time? Imagined crying? The flag they drape over him is so cheap, so flimsy, but not as flimsy as the toilet paper we use to dry our faces. It disintegrates as we cry and laugh into it.

When we finally leave, we notice a patriotic wreath—ribbons and stars and burlap—that some volunteer has hung on the door. We've seen these wreaths migrate from door to door, dead father to dead father. We know it is not ours to take, but we take it. It is the sort of thing our mother would want as a souvenir.

(   )

I have a folder labeled *Dad* where I keep his half-made stories, the ones I read to him on the night he dies. One is a tale of a storm-tossed ship, the inclinometer registering +28%. My father writes:

> *I was happy to stand the mid-watch, and walk out on deck, facing east, just before sunrise. Homer's rosy-fingered dawn was worth the wait and never disappointed. From sheer darkness, other than the ship's running lights, a faintly golden glow perceptibly and gently*

piqued the eastern sky, crept up over the horizon, and emblazoned
the entire ocean view.

That night, I don't read him the parenthetical that comes after, another nod to *Hamlet*, a story of the limits of our vision in the dawn. Instead, I pretend that my father has written the ending. I pretend that the lesson is clear. Loss makes us whole. Grief is care. The Earth is fully formed, a perfect, diggable sphere.

Imagine that. Earth. Ready to bear our weight and light, ready to show us our shadows. See our hands, how they cast dark stars. See our wings, folded, at rest.

ACKNOWLEDGMENTS

Many, many thanks to the folks at Texas Tech University Press and *Iron Horse Literary Review* for loving *Lucky Bodies* and turning it into the book you hold in your hands. Special thanks to Katie Cortese, Leslie Jill Patterson, Travis Snyder, Joanna Conrad, Hannah Gaskamp, Eytan Pol, Christie Perlmutter, and John Brock.

Thanks to the other organizations that have supported the writing of this book, including the National Endowment for the Humanities, the North Carolina Arts Council, The Wake Forest University Humanities Institute, Virginia Center for Creative Arts, and Vermont Studio Center.

I have been honored to first publish earlier versions of some of these essays in the following venues: *Oxford American* ("You Call That Wild"), *Ruminate* ("The Body Is Loyal"), *Michigan Quarterly Review* ("Big Time"), *The Rupture* ("Luck Now"), *Arrowsmith* ("Wolfless"), *Gandy Dancer* ("What the Dead Know by Act Three"), *River Teeth* ("Twenty Wendys"), *Rooted Arboreal Nonfiction Substack* ("The Atonishing"), *The Kenyon Review* ("The Girl the Girls Piece Together"), *storySouth* ("No Sugar"), *The Waking* ("Blueberry Hill"), *Rooted Two: The Best New Arboreal Nonfiction* ("The Taking Boy"), and *Orion* ("The Lark"). So many thanks to the readers and editors at these journals, especially Maxwell George, Jess Jelsma Masterson, Sumanth Prabhaker, and the magical Julia Juster. Thanks, too, to

Laura Gibbs for generously fielding my Aesop questions.

Thank you to my writing teachers and mentors over the years, especially Rachel Hall, Dave Kelly, Jesse Lee Kercheval, Amaud Jamaul Johnson, Judy Mitchell, Belle Boggs, Sabrina Orah Mark, Cyrus Dunham, the late Patricia Lovelock, and the inimitable Sy Safransky.

Many thanks to my writing pals and dear friends, Jess Chevalier and Leah Lavin, for so many shared pages, conversations, and cocktails. You are brilliant and loving guides.

I am indebted to the wisdom of many early readers and champions, especially Chelsey Hillyer, Charlie Espinosa, Anna Peterson, Kate Frazier, Andrea Mummert Puccini, Barbara Leckie, Corinne Casolara, Mary McCarty, Jeff Solomon, Melissa MacLeod, Jamie Maier, my UW–Madison cohort, The Gentle Ghosts at VSC, the VCCA Junebugs, and the moonlit Goddess Circle.

Love and thanks to my family, near and far, especially my father, the late Paul Upham, who gave me a love of books, and my mother, Janet Upham, who gave me a love of stories.

Finally, endless gratitude to my husband Rob and our kids, Nolan and Silas, for loving every draft of me.

ABOUT THE AUTHOR

Marianne Jay Erhardt's writing appears in *Orion*, *Kenyon Review*, *Oxford American*, *Electric Literature*, and *Conjunctions* and has been supported by the National Endowment for the Humanities, the North Carolina Arts Council, Virginia Center for the Creative Arts, and Vermont Studio Center. She holds an MFA from the University of Wisconsin–Madison and teaches writing at Wake Forest University in Winston-Salem, NC, where she lives with her lovely family.

AUTHOR PHOTO BY LIZ NEMETH

WAKE FOREST
U N I V E R S I T Y

The Humanities Institute

NATIONAL ENDOWMENT FOR THE
HUMANITIES

National Endowment for the Humanities Policy Statement

Any views, findings, conclusions, or recommendations expressed in this book do not necessarily represent those of the National Endowment for the Humanities.

www.ingramcontent.com/pod-product-compliance
Lightning Source LLC
Chambersburg PA
CBHW030511230425
25567CB00010B/196/J